THE OTHER SHORE

The Passing Over of Dr. Jack Hyles

DAVID
HYLES

THE OTHER SHORE

The Passing Over of Dr. Jack Hyles

JACK HYLES PRESS
Pinellas Park, Florida

© 2001

JACK HYLES PRESS

Pinellas Park Baptist Temple
4981 - 78th Avenue North
Pinellas Park, Florida 33782

ISBN 097112270-9

WWW.JACKHYLESPRESS.COM

All Scriptures quoted in this text
are from the King James Bible.

Cover Photograph:
Larry Titak, Schererville, Indiana
Courtesy of Eddie Lapina

Family Photograph:
Ruth Sylaidis

The picture on the title page was taken on
January 21, 2001, the last Sunday Brother Hyles
preached at First Baptist Church.

Printed and Bound in the United States of America

DEDICATION

WHEN I WAS A LITTLE boy, I played a game called word association. Someone would say a word, and I would say the first word that came to my mind. For example, if I were to say the word "strawberry," the first word that might come to mind is "shortcake." Perhaps the word used would be "vanilla," and the first words that might come to mind would be "ice cream." I decided to play that game again for a moment. When the name "Jack Hyles" is mentioned, many words come to mind. For example, "Jack Hyles—soul winner." Someone else may say, "Jack Hyles—pastor." Still another might say, "Jack Hyles—others," or "Jack Hyles—giving," or "Jack Hyles—preaching." I believe that the most perfect word answer in that word association game would be, "Jack Hyles—Beverly."

There is no human being who deserves the dedication to this book other than the lady who was Jack Hyles' life. Dad did not say a lot of things in his final days that were heavy. He was careful not to let himself get too emotional. He did not even talk a lot about the church or the ministry. He was perhaps trying not to be fatalistic for himself as much as for all of us.

After Dad died, Mom told me about one serious moment, perhaps the only really, really serious moment or perhaps the

Dedication

most serious statement that Dad made while he was in the hospital. He looked at my mother and said, "You are my whole world."

For that reason, I dedicate this book to my mother who was Jack Hyles' world. To dedicate this book properly, I am going to include in this chapter an article written by me for *Christian Womanhood* in their dedication issue to my dad after he had passed away. It is called, "You Have My Permission." I dedicate this article and this book to the memory of Jack Hyles and to one who was closely associated with him—a lady named "Beverly Hyles," my mom.

———

"You Have My Permission."
by David Hyles

When I was asked if I would like to write an article to honor my dad in the April 2001 issue of the *Christian Womanhood* paper, I sat for a long time and pondered what exactly I would write about my dad. It was and is difficult to know what I should say about him. So much has been said—so much that he deserves. But somehow I felt that I should write not just about Dad, but that I should write about a very special moment at the very end of my dad's life.

I was in Dad's room alone while he was in the hospital. We were talking about his illness and his impending surgery. Dad looked at me and said, "Son, I am not afraid to die. I am ready. I just don't want to leave Mom alone." Several times while Dad was in the hospital, I stood with Mom in his hospital room, and I could see her hand on his, and she would be encouraging him.

The Passing Over of Dr. Jack Hyles

Dad would look at her with a smile that only she received and would lovingly pat her hand. I could feel the love that existed between these two individuals.

I wondered how it must have felt as they both faced the possibility that they would part after 54 years of being together. There were times when I found myself slipping out of the room to leave them alone because I knew there was a special bond that only existed between the two of them. Mom wanted Dad to live. Dad wanted to live for Mom. I don't know that I could give you a sweeter description of what I saw in the hospital than that.

There is something very intimate about what I want to share. It was 12:30 A.M. on February 6. I was asleep at the Residence Inn in Merrillville, Indiana, when the phone rang. It was an intern doctor whose name was Judith calling from the hospital. "Mr. Hyles," she said, "I feel that you and your mother need to come back to the hospital. Your father has taken a turn for the worse, and I think there are some decisions that have to be made." Fear gripped me. "We're losing him," I thought. We knew he was in very critical condition, but we hoped he would make it. I thought, "What do we do? Dad's surgeon said to go home and get some rest. They wouldn't need us until tomorrow." But something inside of me felt I needed to leave this decision up to Mom.

I called her at home. "The hospital called. Dad's taken a turn for the worse, and they have asked us to come."

Her answer startled me. "David, God told me that Dad would die on February 6, and that something would happen shortly after midnight. I gave him to the Lord last night."

You have to understand—I hadn't given him up to the Lord. In fact, I don't think anyone else had given him to the Lord

Dedication

either. I needed him too much. I loved him too much to let him go. My wife and I got dressed, got into the car, and picked up Mom to take her to the hospital. My sister Cindy and her husband Jack joined us shortly. When we arrived, the doctors told us of Dad's severe status. He had gone into cardiac arrest ten or twelve times. They had shocked him back each time. Two emergency code blues had been called before we arrived, signifying that they were losing him, but they brought him back each time. We went into the waiting room and waited.

One male nurse had been assigned to do nothing but try and keep my dad alive. Jack and I went into Dad's room and both privately and then together we spoke into his ear and told him how much we loved him and needed him. It was a horrible sight to see him lying there, hanging between life and death. Cindy came in and begged him to live; she asked him to fight.

Shortly after we arrived, Brother Colsten came. Jack, myself, and Brother Colsten gathered around the bedside and anointed Dad with oil and prayed for God to spare his life. We were not ready to let him go; we loved him too much.

The situation began to look very grim. It looked as though we were about to lose him. Mom didn't fight like the rest of us. We were desperate. She was calm and somewhat resigned. But there was one moment that told it all, and that is the one thing that I want to share. Mom finally came into the room and stood by the side of her companion of 54 years—her best friend. My mother looked down at my dad and said, "I don't want you to go, but it's okay. You can go. You have my permission." Shortly afterward, my dad went into his third code blue. We were rushed from his room. After about 45 minutes, we were told there was no hope. Dad was going to die.

The Passing Over of Dr. Jack Hyles

We loved him too much to let him go, but Mom loved him too much to make him stay. Her love exceeded ours. God had given her an understanding that we did not have. She did not want what was best for her; she wanted what was best for him. Perhaps she was the only one on God's earth who felt that way. I remember coming back into his room while he was still clinging to life. All hope was gone, and while the rest of us cried, Mom began to sing, "In the sweet by and by, We shall meet on that beautiful shore..." I could not sing for I had not let go, but Mom and her lover of life and lifetime lover had something that none of us could possibly have—a love that could say, "I want what's best for you." Perhaps that love was the greatest testimony of their lives.

A few minutes later, Dad's blood pressure began to drop. He did not wait for man to disconnect the machines. He did not need their permission; he had all the permission he needed. His best friend had said, "It's okay; you can go." At 9:43 A.M., February 6, 2001, Jack Hyles breathed his last breath because Beverly Hyles, the love of his life, said, "It's okay; I want what's best for you."

A favorite photo taken on a cruise in 2000

ACKNOWLEDGMENTS

WHEN THIS PROJECT FIRST began, I believe I sensed a skepticism in some regarding its importance. However, it was not long until people began to realize this book had its place and would play an important role in the memorializing of Dr. Jack Hyles. I wish to acknowledge the people who made this book possible. Beyond anyone perhaps would be my mother, Beverly Hyles, who has been an incredible source of inspiration and has rolled up her sleeves and gotten involved in really seeing to it that this book was as well done as it could possibly be.

I wish to thank my wife, Brenda, who not only helped to sort out in my mind the order of events, but also was supportive and encouraging to me to continue pushing forward in writing this book. There were times when it was a very emotional load, and she remained positive and upbeat along with my daughters, Amy and Bethany.

I wish to thank my secretary, Mrs. Julie Roberts, who typed the entire manuscript for me and was a tremendous help in getting this book out expeditiously.

I also wish to acknowledge the help of Rena Fish and Cathy Kimmel with correcting, editing, proofing, and retyping. They did a wonderful job in helping to make this book successful.

Acknowledgments

Thank you, Linda Stubblefield, for your expertise in productions of books, for your opinions, suggestions, ideas, and your devotion to my mother in wanting to see to it that she was pleased in every way while still making sure that this author was happy with his product. You did a marvelous job.

I wish to thank Mrs. Marlene Evans for reading and editing this book and giving several very important suggestions.

There are many others whom I would like to thank, but these are those who diligently helped to see to it that this book was made possible. One other that must not be forgotten is my pastor, Dr. Everett Farris, whose love for my father has caused him to encourage me to do as much as I can to perpetuate the ministry of my father. He is never jealous for my time, but always willing to give up what he might need or want in the best interest of my father's ministry and work. Thank you, Brother Farris, for being my preacher and my friend.

TABLE OF CONTENTS

PREFACE

Just Above the Clouds
by Dave Hyles

"He that observeth the wind shall not sow;
and he that regardeth the clouds shall not reap."
(Ecclesiastes 11:4)

ECAUSE IT WAS AT the last moment, we were unable to get seats together on the airplane for the trip to Indiana to visit my dad in the hospital. My two daughters, Amy and Bethany, sat together in the middle of the plane while my wife Brenda and I sat in the front row of the coach section. Normally, I choose to sit by the aisle, but no aisle seats were available; so Brenda sat in the middle, and I sat by the window. It was an overcast day in Tampa—a stormy looking morning. Even in the darkness of the early hours, a person could see the clouds hovering above. It was the first flight that would leave Tampa on this morning.

The airplane taxied out to the runway and then began to move slowly until accelerating more and more to the point where finally we lifted off the ground and into the air. Almost

Just Above the Clouds

immediately upon takeoff, we were in the clouds. The plane was tossed about a bit to and fro in the turbulence of the morning skies. For several minutes, we continued to rise through the clouds. It was dark, stormy, and cloudy, not just outside, but also in my heart. I did not know what I was about to face, but I was filled with fear. I was not even certain that my dad was still alive.

Finally after several minutes, our plane came through the clouds. No longer were the clouds above us or around us; they were below us. As I could see them still through the dark sky, off in the horizon, the sun was beginning to peak. Its glorious rays would soon lift above the horizon and light the skies above those clouds. After a few minutes of watching the sun come up, suddenly I saw a very glorious, beautiful sight. Below me were pillows of clouds, thick, white, and stunning; off in the distance was the breathtaking morning sun. As I sat in my seat looking out of the window, my heart filled with fear and anticipation of what was to come. A thought came into my mind; it was something my dad had often said when he would talk about his life and how he stayed on "topside," as he would put it. He would often say, "I have lived my life somewhere just a little above the clouds."

I began to cry. The sweetness of that thought turned to the fear of the future. I actually began to wonder if God was laying on my heart that which would be my funeral message for my father. For most of the remainder of the flight, I wept as the entire trip from Tampa, Florida, to Chicago, we flew above a thick bed of billowy clouds. As we flew, I thought about my dad's life; somehow Dad *had* managed to walk just a bit above the clouds. He did not live his life under the clouds like most people; he lived life above them to where he could see the sun. Perhaps

The Passing Over of Dr. Jack Hyles

there is nothing that describes the ability that my dad had to be happy like the statement, "I have lived my life somewhere just a little above the clouds."

He lived his life a little above the clouds of betrayal when those who had once called themselves friends turned their backs on him. He lived a little above the clouds of criticism and slander when people judged his heart, his motives, and his actions unjustly. He lived a little above the clouds of attacks by enemies who sought to destroy his prosperous ministry. He lived a little above the clouds of goodbyes as he parted from loved ones or loved ones parted from him. He lived a little above the clouds of death that had oft greeted him in his 74 years of life.

He lived a little above the clouds of gossip, not only about himself, but also about others whom he loved. He lived a little above the clouds of hatred even though in his heart he was truly a lover, yet still he managed to rise above those clouds of hatred and not allow those clouds to cover the sunshine in his heart. He lived a little above the clouds of false accusations by those who chose to make unscriptural accusations against him that were not true. He lived a little above the clouds of controversy that often swirled about him not because of something he had done wrong, but because of the principles by which he lived so carefully.

He walked a little above the clouds of loneliness as he walked through many airports and slept alone in many hotels, trying to do what he could for God. He lived a little above the clouds of weariness as he worked tirelessly to help others. He lived a little above the clouds of separation as he spent so many nights away from the love of his life, his own wife.

He lived a little above the clouds of pain and sickness as for

Just Above the Clouds

years he managed to overcome the pain that was more excruciating than any of us knew as he continued to do the work that God had sent him to do. He lived a little above the clouds of doubt and fear while others trembled from circumstances. He refused to allow circumstances to draw him under the cloud. He lived a little above the clouds of disappointments from people who simply let him down. He lived a little above the clouds of injustice that often surfaced against him by preachers as well as former church members who chose to act as judge and jury.

These clouds could not cast a shadow on him because he walked above them, not below them. The rain they sent fell to where only his shadow stood because he stood above these clouds. Their winds blew where he should have walked, but their winds could not have hit him for he walked above the clouds. While the darkness covered the earth below, he was seeing the sunshine above!

The clouds were not his ceiling but his carpeting; they were not his sky but his footstool. The clouds did not cover his light but cushioned his feet. These clouds did not hover ominously about him but lay innocently below him. They were not stormy burdens but ways of peace.

So how did he help so many who were overcome by clouds? This perhaps was the greatness of Jack Hyles: he did not come down under their clouds to encourage them; he lifted them up above to where he walked above the clouds. Preachers brought Jack Hyles to their churches to preach, not so that he could walk with them under their clouds, but so he could lift them and their churches above the clouds that had hovered above their churches and ministries. When he walked into the pulpit of First Baptist Church of Hammond, he somehow managed to lift thousands

The Passing Over of Dr. Jack Hyles

above the clouds so they could see the sunshine. The lines of people who stood outside of his office for counseling often did not come in order to figure out how to find an umbrella for the rain in their lives, but rather to find a journey above the rain and above the clouds.

Somehow, though the clouds constantly tried to hover above him, he always managed to climb a ladder of belief and faith to a place above those clouds where he could see the sun rather than feel the storm.

In March of 1999, a monsoon came into his life. In one day, he discovered that he had a heart disease; and on that same day, my son, his grandson and his namesake, Jack David Hyles, died. The thick, dark clouds, more menacing perhaps than any that had ever come into his life, gathered in his way. How could he go on? There was only one way. He had to do what he had done for all of those many years; he had to climb the stairway of faith again and walk above those menacing clouds. How could he be so sick and yet go on? He was walking just a little above the clouds. How could he lose his grandson and go on? He was walking just a little above the clouds.

It is interesting to me that on the day of his viewing, the day where thousands would walk by and see his body lying in state in the First Baptist Church of Hammond, Indiana, it was a cloudy, gloomy, stormy day. Death had cast its shadow over all of us. I felt a sense of gloom that day as the clouds took away our sunshine. Saturday morning, the day of his funeral, the day the casket would be placed into the crypt, I awoke and looked out the window of our hotel room; and there were no clouds in the sky—only the beautiful sunshine. There was a mourning group of Christians across the country and the world, a mourning

Just Above the Clouds

church, and a mourning family. I believe that somehow from Heaven, with God's permission, Dad was lifting up the clouds that had so covered them for several days to where we could see the sun shine once again.

When Dad was in the hospital, he talked to me about the fact that he had been a busy man, and he had not had the time to spend with his grandchildren. To my niece and to me privately, he said, "Son, no matter what happens, even if I am not able to go on with my ministry, when I get out of this hospital, I think I could enjoy just being a grandpa."

As he lay in the hospital, the clouds of death hovered above him, but once again the clouds failed to land a shadow on their intended target. For somewhere far above the clouds, Dr. Jack Hyles was running down the streets of gold with his little grandson, Jack David, on his shoulders—just being a grandpa.

INTRODUCTION

Home Really Is a Person
by Beverly Hyles

AST OCTOBER 2000, BROTHER Hyles spoke at the *Christian Womanhood* Spectacular on the subject, "Home Is a Person." Because I knew he was honoring me, I don't think I listened too carefully or with my "heart."

Now that message has been made a reality to me.

At this writing, two years ago, during the spring of 1999, we sold our home of 40 years and bought a condominium. The main reason was to give my husband peace that should he go to Heaven before I did, I wouldn't have the care of a big home, yard, etc.

We looked at several places, but as he said, when we walked into the one that would be "it," my eyes sparkled.

We had so much fun decorating it together and for almost two years enjoyed living in it. We said often how right it was and how much we loved it.

As you enter, you see our dining room in which we enjoyed meals and holidays with family. In this area are two of my

Home Really Is a Person

paintings put there at his insistence. He was such a cheerleader for my accomplishments—meals, decorating for holidays, singing, painting. He just made me feel anything I did was great!

Then you enter our spacious living room where we loved to sit together and talk or read the paper—often with a beautiful cd playing softly. Nearly every night he would say, "Time for the love seat!" We would just sit together before retiring and enjoy fully each other's presence.

The south end of our living room is a wall of windows, floor to ceiling, that leads to a glassed-in porch which we used both summer and winter. He loved the porch. Often he took his books and studied there. We have a little dining table and two stools, and very often, we had our breakfast on the porch as we watched squirrels play in the huge oak trees just outside.

From our kitchen, you enter the smaller of the two bedrooms which we made into a bedroom/den. Left of this room is his bathroom and walk-in closet with neat lines of beautiful suits, shoes, shirts, and the faint smell of Coty Musk for Men. It reminds me of his fastidiousness and very good grooming.

Across the condo on the opposite side is our large bedroom and my bath which is unusually large and feminine, and to him, it was designed for me.

I, too, have a walk-in closet full of beautiful clothes, nearly all of which he bought for me or shopped with me to purchase.

Our bedroom reminds me of so many nights in early 2001 when he had to sit up in a chair because of pain in his back left shoulder or just below the breastbone. But how many nights I awoke to realize he was there beside me—not out of town preaching. How peaceful it felt.

I still live in Sand Oaks Condominiums, number 204. It's

The Passing Over of Dr. Jack Hyles

still lovely. But my "home" is gone.

This morning the first thing I saw as I opened my curtains was a squirrel playing in an oak, but it didn't seem the same.

I fixed myself a light breakfast and took it to the porch. Something—someone—was missing. My morning grooming took place, but no one said, "There's my pretty girl." I wondered, "Why did I bother?"

As I write this, I am sitting in my comfortable living room with the cd "Theme from Anne of Green Gables" playing. It is both beautiful and sad at the same time. My husband was the home to me, and I was that to him.

I am so glad I regularly was his cheerleader, telling him how great his sermons were, or how they helped me. I took careful notice of how much time he spent in preparation (usually when I was busy). We both took the time when we could to just be together.

The silly, fun times we had together playing games, or calling each other "pet" names, or when each morning breakfast was ready, I would sing, "I need a handsome man." He always replied, "I can't find one." We didn't always feel like being "light," but we did it!

When I walked out of our condo with my suitcases to go on two summer cruises and two trips to Hawaii, I took my home with me. We had the same fun.

The last trip to Hawaii ended on Saturday, January 20, 2001. The following Saturday, my husband went to the emergency room to see his doctor because his pain wouldn't ease. The following Tuesday, January 30, he entered the hospital where he was put into ICU.

I'll never forget that evening when the nurse said, "Call the

Home Really Is a Person

family; he's critical." Critical isn't a word for "home."

In the early morning hours of Friday, February 2, my "home" was airlifted to a Chicago Hospital where he was to be "stabilized" for open-heart surgery. The surgery was performed on Monday, February 5, lasting eight hours. At 9:43 A.M., Tuesday, February 6, my "home" went to be with Jesus.

Yes, I can testify. Home is a person.

INTRODUCTION

The Other Shore
by David Hyles

N MARCH 24, 1999, my son, Jack David, went to Heaven. At the time my son passed away, my life changed forever. I felt grief that I never dreamed I could feel. I still remember having heard people say, "My heart aches," and I discovered that it was a true statement. My heart literally ached at the loss of my son.

At the time of my son's death, I taught a Sunday school class called the New Life Bible Class. That class rallied behind my family and me in an incredible way. They were there for us every time we needed them. I had a Sunday school paper called the *Life Lines* that I gave to my class every week. When Jack David died, every Sunday I wrote articles about Jack David and shared what was happening in our lives as we remembered him. My class relished these articles; my writing drew them close to me and was a blessing to them. Also, writing these articles was a tremendous therapy for me. Perhaps what helped me to endure the first six months of my son's being gone was being able to share it with my Sunday school class through my articles.

The Other Shore

On February 6, 2001, my dad, Jack Hyles, went to Heaven. It was less than two years after the death of my son. Once again my life was changed; and once again I became acquainted with grief.

Two circumstances inspired this book: I was inspired, first of all, by the fact that so many people loved my dad and were devastated with the suddenness of his departure. Everyone was shocked. On one Wednesday night, Dad was teaching a Bible study at the First Baptist Church of Hammond; and two Wednesday nights later, the church was without a pastor. He was there, and then he was gone. I felt people needed to know what happened.

The second reason for writing this book was a very selfish reason; I simply needed to write it. It was therapy to me. Strangely enough, when my mother first read this manuscript, she too said, "I needed this book. It made me cry, and I needed to release those tears." Writing helped me to relive and to make sense of the events that led to Dad's death.

These two reasons caused me to work on this book diligently in the first few weeks after Dad was gone. I knew I needed to write it, and I knew those who loved Dad needed to know what had happened.

Another consideration in the writing of this book was whether or not it would simply be a book of facts or a book of principles Dad had taught in his life. I felt this book would honor Dad by allowing him to teach through his death because he died teaching the principles by which he had lived. Those principles were exhibited throughout the two weeks before his death. What a man he was, and how proud I am to write about the greatness of not just his life, but the greatness of his death.

The Passing Over of Dr. Jack Hyles

November 25, 2000, less than three months before Dad would die, he preached a great sermon called "The Other Shore." Shortly after Dad died, Mom found that sermon and listened to it. In the sermon, he talked about those who were waiting on the Other Shore. He said that sometimes he felt like he had one foot on this side and one foot on the Other Shore. He talked about those who were waiting for him on the Other Shore. Though he loved life, there was already a sense of looking ahead to the time he would step across the river to the Other Shore called Heaven.

When we began to decide what we would call this book, I struggled with titles. Do you call it *The Death of Dr. Jack Hyles?* No doubt, that title would be too morbid. What words exactly described what I was about to write? When Mom told me about listening to the sermon, shortly thereafter the idea came to call it, *The Other Shore: The Passing Over of Dr. Jack Hyles.* For you see, that was really all it was. Dad lived his life looking across and seeing what was awaiting him as he continued to do the work that God gave him to do here on earth. He never planned on leaving quite this quickly, but he was ready when his time came to make that crossing over.

Much has been written in poetry and in notes and cards about what it must have been like when Dad got to Heaven. Some suggested that he ignored all whom he loved and went straight to Jesus. Some suggested that those he loved ignored him and pointed him toward Jesus. I am not sure exactly what happened when Dad crossed over to the Other Shore, but this much I can tell you, I believe that Dad took that step across with mixed emotions—happy to be there and sad to be leaving. I believe a great host of people were waiting for him, and I think

The Other Shore

that Jesus was in the midst of them. I do not believe it was a choice between seeing Jesus and seeing loves ones. I like to think they were all waiting together. They knew Jesus well enough to just be part of that welcoming committee.

When Jack David died, my wife asked me a question one day that quite frankly surprised me. She asked, "David, I know Heaven is wonderful, but do you think Jack David misses you and me and his sisters?" I had to think about that question for a while. "When you get to Heaven, is it so wonderful that you do not miss the ones you love?" I wondered. After some thought, this was my answer. When we are here on earth, there is a desire to be here. As great as Heaven must be and as much as we miss the people there, we want to be here even though our hearts yearn deeply to see those we love. Is it a sin to yearn for them? No! It is not a sin; it is the natural feeling we have for those we love. Jesus even anticipated our coming to Him. He talked about leaving us, giving us a Comforter, and preparing a place. These promises make it obvious to me that He is anticipating our coming.

I believe Jack David and Jack Hyles miss us all in Heaven right now. I believe he misses First Baptist Church of Hammond. I believe Jack Hyles misses his preacher friends. I believe he misses his staff and the students in his schools. I believe he misses his children and his grandchildren. Most of all, I believe he misses the one person in his life he loved the most, Beverly Joyce Hyles. It is wonderful in Heaven, and he certainly is enjoying the presence of those he loved as he anticipated going there. He is glad to be there, but he certainly does miss us, and I imagine he speaks the same now as he spoke then.

On November 25, 2000, Jack Hyles stood on the shore of

The Passing Over of Dr. Jack Hyles

earth, looked on the other side, and saw those awaiting him. He longed to see them, while he did not long to leave this place. Today, at this very moment, Jack Hyles stands on the other side in Heaven and now looks across to this side and sees all those he loves and misses them and wishes they were with him. Even so, he would not be anxious to leave where he is now. For when Jack Hyles stepped across, he stepped across having loved those of us he was leaving behind and being reunited with the ones he loved who had gone on ahead. You see, all he really did was leave one congregation of people he loved and went to another congregation of people he loved. The same Jack Hyles with the same love is just on another shore!

1

Our Story

"But he that is greatest among you shall be your servant."
(Matthew 23:11)

URPRISINGLY, PERHAPS THE BEST description of the Homegoing of my father came from the local newspaper. *The Hammond Times* which had been, for the most part, antagonistic to Dr. Hyles wrote: "The Reverend Jack Hyles did the unthinkable Tuesday. The man who, for more than forty years was a driving force spiritually and educationally to an uncountable tally of followers in Northwest Indiana and the country, died Tuesday morning at The University of Chicago Hospitals." Those words immediately followed the headline in the newspaper on Wednesday, February 7, 2001, the day after my dad went to be with the Lord.

The next paragraph of the paper read, "His death was a stunning blow, as the 74-year-old pastor of First Baptist Church of Hammond and founder of Hyles-Anderson College led his

The Passing Over of Dr. Jack Hyles

congregation with all the zeal of a freshly starched, spit-shine polished graduate of Bible school."

"Stunning" is the best word to describe my dad's death. In fact, if you had asked anyone who learned of Dad's death how he felt, inevitably the answer used the word, "stunned."

It was at 9:43 A.M., Tuesday, February 6, that my dad struggled for and breathed his last breath of life before entering into Heaven. The events that led to that moment deserve to be more than just a footnote in the biography of his life. Thus came the decision to chronicle in great detail the last days and weeks of my dad's life. I never dreamed of writing such a book; but shortly after Dad died, I felt that it was necessary for people to know more of the story in an attempt to help bring some finality to losing someone whom they had loved and looked to so greatly.

Dad was a great leader, but more than that, he was a great servant. His life touched hundreds of thousands of people across this nation and across the world. People were so stunned at hearing of his death because no one expected it. Jack Hyles just was not supposed to die this soon nor this quickly. There was no real warning of his death, at least not a warning that most people could see. It seemed almost like it could not be true. I suppose that perhaps few deaths in the history of the Christian world came more as an abrupt end to a man's ministry than did Dad's death. It seemed there were so many things he had started, so many things that he had yet to do. In many ways, he was still in the prime of his ministry—not the end.

The ministries of Dr. Jack Hyles and the First Baptist Church were embarking upon some new exciting endeavors. A brand new $4,000,000 educational facility was in the works. Many new and exciting plans were being undertaken at all the

Our Story

schools. In fact, it almost seemed as though Dad had found a new lease on life as he embarked upon many new projects and while he continued to build with great zeal. However, there was more behind the story than most people could see; Dad was a very, very ill man.

In March of 1999, Dad conducted the annual Pastors' School at First Baptist Church of Hammond, Indiana. He spoke in every session, and his 72-year-old body was tested and over-tested to its limits. When Pastors' School ended, Dad was physically as well as emotionally exhausted. For almost four years preceding this, Dad had been bothered by severe pain between the shoulder blades in his back. The pain would come and go but was definitely a discomfort to him. This time it was so bad that he could hardly recover.

Sometimes when Dad arrived at an airport, he would ask to go to the restroom simply so that he could rest a moment and try to eliminate some of that nagging pain. He dismissed the pain for a long time; but after Pastors' School ended, it was overbearing and overpowering to him. He decided that he needed to know exactly what was causing this pain.

The week following the 1999 Pastors' School, Dad admitted himself into Mayo Clinic in Rochester, Minnesota, to go through a series of tests to try to find out exactly what was causing his severe pain. This decision was unlike Dad, but the pain had become so bad that he knew something must be wrong; and he wanted to find out, if he could, some answers.

The Mayo Clinic is one of the greatest medical facilities in the world. It is basically famous for its ability to diagnose what is wrong with someone. They ran extensive tests on Dad in an attempt to find out exactly what was wrong with him. He was

The Passing Over of Dr. Jack Hyles

there for several days, going through these many tests.

On Wednesday, March 24, 1999, the doctors finally came to Dad with some results. Dad was informed that he had a problem with his heart. A valve was not functioning properly, and that was causing some of his health problems. The doctors told him that this was not necessarily a life-threatening problem, although surgery was suggested. They also gave him the option of taking medication to try to eliminate the problem. However, the diagnosis was a major blow to Dad. He realized his heart was bad, and he was faced with a very difficult decision. He later referred to that time as one of the lowest days of his life.

Later that same evening, while Dad was lying there somewhat feeling sorry for himself, he received the phone call that our son Jack David had died. Perhaps no day had been filled with more sorrow in his entire life than this one day.

The following Monday, Mom and Dad flew to Florida for the funeral of our son. They were here just long enough for the service and then rushed to the airport where they flew back to the Mayo Clinic in Minnesota for some follow up concerning Dad's health. My family flew to Chicago on Wednesday. Friday we had a graveside service and placed our son in a crypt at Memory Lane Cemetery owned by First Baptist Church. Dad was not in the pulpit that Wednesday night, but he came back in town the next day for the burial of our son.

To be sure, Dad had some very difficult decisions facing him. This may have been one of the most crucial times of Dad's entire life. He had several decisions to make. Would he have heart surgery and try to repair what was wrong with his heart? Would he just go on and try to continue the best that he could without the surgery? He was also dealing with the decision of where he

Our Story

and my mom would live. Dad had even been discussing with Mom the possibility of retiring and leaving the Hammond area, basically so that he would not be in the way of the next pastor. If they stayed in Hammond, he and Mom had considered buying a condominium and selling the home where they had been for 40 years. These were just a few important decisions, all of which would have a great affect on the future.

One of the first decisions Dad made was to stay in Hammond. He felt it would be unfair to make Mom leave where she had lived all these years and be away from friends of a lifetime. Dad bought a condominium in Munster, Indiana, the city where they had lived for over 40 years. They had looked at this condominium together and had liked it, but they were not yet sure if it was the right decision. When Dad decided to stay in the area, he felt that this was an important move for them. One day, he came home to surprise her and said, "You now own a condominium."

In May of 1999, I was speaking at the Soul Winning Clinic at Longview Baptist Temple. Dad was also there preaching. Brenda and I visited him in his motel room, and he sat us down and told us the news that they were selling the house where we had been reared. He felt that the devastation of losing our son and of their selling the house would be very hard for us, so he wanted to break the news to us gently. God had already prepared my heart. That which I thought would break my heart was not really a big matter. I had great inner peace concerning the decision they had made. A few weeks later, Mom and Dad packed up their belongings of 40 years and moved into a beautiful new condominium. As I look back at that decision, I realize God led my Dad to move my Mom into a place of security

The Passing Over of Dr. Jack Hyles

where, two years later, she would need to be after he was gone.

Another decision Dad made was not to have surgery. I will address this decision in another chapter of this book and describe more of my feelings, but I am convinced that God laid this decision on my Dad's heart because it was best. Dad would go on and continue to preach and do all that he had been doing and leave the rest in the hands of God. I believe that God gave my Dad a complete peace concerning this decision.

The next decision Dad made was to stay as pastor of First Baptist Church for as long as possible. He let the church, the college, and all of the other ministries know that he was there to stay; and he would continue to serve them in whatever capacity possible for the rest of his life. His promise seemed to bring a tremendous calming effect to First Baptist Church.

Dad worked very hard to stay healthy after this diagnosis. He took vitamins and supplements. He watched his diet very carefully. He kept on going and doing as much as he could. He preached with great, renewed power. His messages seemed to have a new sense of depth and insight. God's hand was certainly upon him.

The two years between the time he was diagnosed with a heart disease and the time that he went to Heaven were two of the richest years of his life. Dad accomplished so much in his final two years. He and Mom enjoyed some of their sweetest times together. They enjoyed each other's company more than ever. They took a number of trips together as well as a couple of cruises. They thoroughly enjoyed the time they had to be alone together.

One area in which Dad did slow down was in his travels. He continued to preach conferences, but on a somewhat limited

Our Story

scale. He began going out of town every other week to preach, and eventually he canceled morning sessions and only preached in the evenings. He was doing his best to take good care of himself, yet he was continuing almost all that he had always done in his ministry.

I had the privilege of taking a trip with my dad to San Antonio, Texas, less than a year before he died. He was different on this trip than he had ever been. Many times when I would go with Dad, he would spend a lot of time working; and we would squeeze in a little time together. On this particular trip, he was more focused on me. I remember on Monday afternoon taking a long walk with him. We went into a little deli and had a Coke together. We talked about everything under the sun. When Dad and I were together, we loved to philosophize. We had a great time sharing thoughts about philosophy, especially biblical philosophy. That night we watched the Los Angeles Lakers and the Portland Trail Blazers play basketball on television. It was the playoffs. It had been many years since Dad and I had sat down and watched a game together. We had a good time. We were just going to watch a few minutes, and we ended up watching the entire game. That time was something I will never forget.

The next day we spent a large amount of time together walking and talking. Dad was suffering tremendously with his back. He would stop every once in a while and say, "Son, I just need to stop and lean on something." We would take five minutes for him to get a little relief. We would walk a little more, and then we would have to stop again. Dad was obviously suffering with the pain in his back. The trip was something that I treasure now more than ever. It was a delight to have the

The Passing Over of Dr. Jack Hyles

opportunity of being with my dad.

In November, I again had the opportunity to spend time with Dad. He was preaching in Orange Park, Florida, for one of his dearest friends, Dr. Tom Neal, and he asked me to drive up and spend Tuesday morning with him. The trip was interesting in many ways. Dad talked about the future of First Baptist Church. He told me that he had decided not to groom any successor, and that he had no one in mind to pastor First Baptist after his death. I thought it was a bit strange that he was talking about this, but now I wonder if somehow he knew that the end of his ministry might be near. It was again obvious to me that Dad was suffering from back pain. We spent several hours together talking about the condition of Fundamentalism. One of the things my dad said to me that day was particularly of great interest to me. He asked, "Son, who is going to think for our guys after I am gone?" Again, it seemed that Dad was looking ahead with a certain knowledge that maybe his ministry and even his life was near the end.

In December of 2000, Dad was scheduled to preach at our church, Pinellas Park Baptist Temple, in Pinellas Park, Florida. Dad was scheduled every winter at the beginning of the Christmas season for our Winter Bible Conference. It was always an encouraging kind of conference. Preachers and churches from all over the area would come and find a tremendous amount of encouragement. Mom was going to come with him so we could spend some time together for Christmas. The Monday morning of the conference, I received word that there was a blizzard in the Chicago area. I feared that Dad might not be able to come. Around noon we finally received news that O'Hare Airport had been closed. Dad's secretary called to cancel the meeting. My

Our Story

wife wept when she found out that he was not coming. She said to me, "David, why did God stop him from coming? Something is wrong. Why did God not let him come?" I did not tell her, but I also had a strange feeling about it though I could not explain why. There was just something unnerving about the whole situation, and we felt a need to be with Mom and Dad.

A couple of weeks later, I was out soul winning on a Saturday. My cell phone rang; it was my wife. She said, "David, there was a message on our phone from last night. It was from your mom. She called to tell us that she and Dad decided that since they could not see us at the conference, they were going to catch a plane and fly to Florida just to spend the day with us." I was so excited; I could not believe that my parents

A snapshot taken of Mom and Dad during their visit

were going to come just for a visit. You have to understand that Dad was so busy that he seldom had the time to do something like that. We were so excited about their coming. We anticipated having a day to spend with Mom and Dad. Looking back upon it, I praise God for the opportunity even more.

January 1, 2001, in the late afternoon, my parents arrived at the Tampa International Airport. We greeted Mom and Dad as they got off the airplane. We did not take them the fastest way,

The Passing Over of Dr. Jack Hyles

but we took them a longer, more scenic way. The sun was setting, and my parents talked about how beautiful it was. We took them to their motel for a few minutes and then went out to dinner together. What a wonderful evening!

The next day, we went to Bob Evans for breakfast and then just drove around the area. We took them to see some alligators. Dad didn't want to get out of the car because he said it was too cold, but I think it was because he was scared of the alligators. We drove to an orange grove and bought some freshly squeezed orange juice and an orange ice cream cone. Then we drove down Gulf Boulevard for them to see all the beautiful homes and tourist spots on the ocean front. Dad commented how beautiful it was. Later we stopped at McDonald's and bought a Coke and sat for a long time talking. Mom and Dad had given us a cruise for Christmas; we talked about where we would go. Dad was excited about helping us plan the cruise. The last thing he said as we sat there at McDonald's was, "Be sure to let me know, and I will help make all the arrangements." Dad was so pleased to be able to help us with this.

Late that afternoon we took them back to the airport. As usual we took them to the curb of the departure terminal. Mom and Dad never liked to be walked to the gate; they wanted their goodbyes to be short and sweet. I got out of the car, opened the trunk, and took out their bags. I hugged my Mom and shook Dad's hand and thanked him for coming. I told him I loved him as I always did, and he told me that he loved me; then they turned and walked away. When I got back in the car, I was gripped with a fear that something was not right. Brenda said the same thing. She said, "I hope that is not the last time we see him." Something about it caused us to be afraid and to wonder

Our Story

if there was a reason that God had allowed this mini-vacation to happen.

A few days later, Mom and Dad went on a ten-day trip to Hawaii. I talked to Mom about it after Dad died. She said, "It was a wonderful time." She could tell at times that Dad was in pain; but for the most part, they really enjoyed themselves. They stayed in their favorite place in Hawaii, a hotel overlooking the ocean. When they went to Hawaii, they did not do much sight seeing. It was a great vacation for them—a time they thoroughly enjoyed together. I asked Mom if she felt anything was different on the trip. She said, "Dad was in a lot of pain from time to time, but he slept fairly well. Sometimes during the night he would have to get up and sit for a while to relieve the pain in his back. Then he was able to go back and lie down and get some rest." Their final vacation was a sweet time for the two of them.

They flew back into town on Saturday, January 20, 2001. The next morning, Dad preached in the pulpit of First Baptist Church. It was to be his final Sunday. Sunday morning the title of his sermon was, "God the Espier." Sunday night's sermon was entitled, "Don't Call Me, I'll Call You." They were both great messages, vintage Jack Hyles. The next morning Dad was scheduled to go to Monterey, Mexico, to preach in a Fundamentalist Conference. He boarded a plane and flew that great distance along with several of the men in the Fundamentalist Conference Committee.

Dad preached three times while he was in Monterey. Monday night he preached a great, powerful sermon that was somewhat shorter than what Dad usually preached. He again preached on Tuesday morning, but the Tuesday night service would prove to be the most difficult. During the service on

The Passing Over of Dr. Jack Hyles

Tuesday night, he was smitten with what we later believed to be a heart attack. The pain was excruciating as though this were the final hurrah. When he was finished preaching, he said to himself, "That is it; I am finished." Dad did not sleep at all that night, both because of the pain and the fear that if he went to sleep, he would not awaken. He was scared that he was going to die not because he feared death, but because he was not yet ready to say goodbye to Mom. Throughout the night, he worked and prepared for the possibility that his life might be over.

The next day Dad flew back to Indiana. He had not spoken to Mom since he had left on Monday morning. When he came through the door at home, she sensed that something was wrong. She said, "How was the meeting?" He said, "Let me unpack my bags; then we will sit down, and I'll tell you all about it." In a few minutes, Dad would give to Mom all the details of the meeting and reveal to her the severity of his pain. This was to be the final evening that Dad would ever preach in the pulpit of the First Baptist Church of Hammond, and this would begin a series of days that would lead to the end of his life.

CHAPTER

2

The Final Service

*"For I am now ready to be offered,
and the time of my departure is at hand."*
(II Timothy 4:6)

AD UNPACKED HIS BAGS and put away his things. He went into the living room, sat down with Mom, and told her what had happened in Monterey, Mexico. It was obvious that Dad was suffering terribly. Mom was alarmed to say the least. One thing that Dad did not want was to have any heart exams. Perhaps he knew that the moment he had the exam, it would be the end; and he was not ready for the end. Though he was in pain and feared what had happened to him in Monterey, he decided to go ahead and do his business as best he could.

That night, Dad conducted his final teachers' and officers' meeting. He also conducted his final superintendents' meeting. He then went into the auditorium of the First Baptist Church of

The Passing Over of Dr. Jack Hyles

Hammond and led in his final Wednesday night service. In fact, it proved to be his final service ever at the First Baptist Church of Hammond. Before going out to the platform that night, he said to some of the men on the staff, "Fellows, you better get a plan ready for Pastors' School without me. I am not sure that I am going to be well enough to be there." It is amazing how prophetic that statement would be.

That night he slept fairly well, although he got up several times during the night and had to sit up for a while because of the pain. It was one of the last nights that he would actually sleep lying down in his bed at home.

The next morning he went to work and tried to conduct business as usual, but it was obvious he was not feeling well. Not only was he in constant back pain, he had also developed some kind of infection in his lungs. To top it off, he had gained a couple of pounds; and there seemed to be no logical reason for this weight gain. This gain particularly alarmed Mom, so she decided to call Mrs. Kris Grafton, Dad's nurse, to tell her a little bit about what was happening with Dad. Mrs. Grafton called Dad's doctor, Dr. Dennis Streeter, who suggested that Dad come in and go through a series of tests to see if they could find out what was wrong.

On Friday, their usual date day, Mom told Dad that Dr. Streeter wanted to see him. To begin their date, Dad always picked up Mom for lunch, and they would go to Burger King and get their standard order—Whopper Juniors minus mayonnaise, plus mustard and two medium diet Cokes. Then they would drive to a park to eat. Each week they would take turns choosing three restaurants, and the other one would choose from one of those three for their date night dinner. On this day, there was a

The Final Service

damper on their date. Dad was upset that Mom had called the doctor. He was not angry, but he was frustrated. Finally, he agreed to go to the doctor, but he still refused to allow them to run any heart tests. They finished their evening and their date, but it was obvious that Dad was troubled at the thought of going to the doctor.

I was sitting in my office on Saturday around noon. My cell phone rang; it was my pastor. He said, "Brother Dave, I do not want you to get alarmed, but I just got word that your dad was rushed to the hospital. You might want to call and see what you can find out." I immediately started making phone calls. It seemed that everyone I called knew nothing about what was happening. Finally, about 3:00 on Saturday afternoon I was able to reach my brother-in-law, Jack Schaap. He informed me that Dad had gone to the emergency room at the hospital for a prearranged appointment with Dr. Streeter. He had canceled all his meetings and appointments for the day. He said that he had not yet received any news, but as soon as he found out something, he would let me know.

The alarm was false; yet it was partially true. Dad had gone in to have some tests performed. Late that afternoon, I was finally able to reach Mom and chat with her for a couple of minutes. She told me that the doctor had found some kind of infection in Dad's lungs, but he had not allowed them to do any heart tests. The doctor had also found some irritation on Dad's back and thought that it might be shingles. That was later explained; Mom had put a heating pad on Dad's back to try to help him get some relief from his pain, and that had caused some severe irritation. The doctor also thought it might be arthritis in his back causing part of the problem. Several probable solutions

The Passing Over of Dr. Jack Hyles

were offered but nothing yet about the heart, because Dad had refused to allow them to run the tests.

Later that evening, when I talked to Dad, I could tell he was sick. His words were labored. In fact, Mom did not think he would be able to talk because of the pain he was experiencing. Dad knew that I was alarmed and many miles away, and he wanted to assure me that he was okay. We only talked for a few minutes. He said, "Son, I am in severe pain, but I think I'll be fine. The doctor has given me something for the pain as well as a shot of cortisone in my back. He even told me that if I felt better I could probably preach tomorrow. The way I feel right now though, I am not sure I am going to be able to." His breathing was very labored, and he talked very slowly and deliberately. I could tell that he was not doing very well at all.

The cortisone shots and the prescribed medication did not help at all. Dad's pain was excruciating and constant. He could no longer lie down; he had to sit up to sleep. He was in tremendous discomfort. He never even considered going to church the next day, much less preaching. He was very ill, and now he feared there might be some type of infection in his lungs.

I called that afternoon to check on him. Mom said, "David, Dad is very sick. I am terribly worried about him. I know he is sick because he has not even wanted to study or work on sermons. He has not even picked up his Bible and tried to read. He is just sitting in his chair in a horrible pain." Mom's voice carried an obvious tone of worry.

Tuesday morning I again called to see how Dad was doing. Mom said, "Son, Dad is still extremely sick. I called the doctor, and we are going to have some tests run this afternoon. He may have pneumonia in his lungs, and we want to see if we can find

The Final Service

out if that is causing part of his problems." Then she made a statement that brought fear to me. She said, "Son, he is gaining weight. It is apparently fluid because he cannot eat. I know that is one sign of congestive heart failure."

The appointment was scheduled for 3:00 that afternoon. Around 6:00 that evening I began to call my parents' house, but there was no answer. The next three hours I called over and over again, trying to reach them. Finally I began to call my sister Cindy's home, but I was unable to reach her. At about 10:00 that night, I finally received a call from Mrs. Farris, my pastor's wife, informing me that my sister had been trying to get in touch with me; and that it was important for me to call them at a hospital pay phone. Apparently they only had my cell phone number with them, and my cell phone was off. I immediately called and talked to my sister Cindy. She said, "Dad has had a heart attack. He is in intensive care. The doctors say that the family needs to come now."

That afternoon they had run diagnostic tests and discovered that Dad had indeed suffered a heart attack. He was in critical condition. When the doctor first talked to my Mom, he had indicated that Dad was very sick but had not really indicated how severe it was. When the doctor left the room, a nurse made it very clear. She told Mom that all of the family members should be contacted, and she suggested that they needed to come immediately. Though the extent of the severity of his condition was not yet clear, there was no question that Dad was going to have a long and difficult road ahead.

We learned that apparently Dad had been right about his suffering a heart attack the previous Tuesday night in Monterey, Mexico. He had tried to keep going for as long as he could, but

The Passing Over of Dr. Jack Hyles

his condition was very severe; and the debilitating effects finally overcame him. He was always a fighter, but for now he was losing this fight.

Our family members began to arrive for what would be the final days of Dad's life. His sister Earlyne came that night and joined Mom, my sister Cindy, and her husband Jack. The four of them would keep vigil all night that first night Dad was in the hospital. I spent several hours trying to get flights to Chicago. Finally, we were able to locate tickets to leave on the very first flight that left Florida for Chicago the next morning. We tried to sleep, but we had to be up at about 3:00 in the morning in order to catch our flight, and it was already well after midnight. Sleep failed us as we worried about Dad. Little did we realize the severity of Dad's condition. In fact, I am not sure anybody realized it at this point. Dad was graded in very critical condition. The doctors feared they might lose him during the night. At this time, even Dad was not yet aware of just how terribly ill he was.

When we got on the airplane the next morning, I did not know whether or not we would find Dad alive when we landed. I believe my greatest fear was that I would get off the airplane and learn that he was already gone. I wept the entire flight to Chicago. A dear friend, Keith McKinney, picked us up at the airport and drove us straight to the Broadway Methodist Hospital. He assured me that Dad was alive, more tests were being scheduled to find out exactly what was wrong.

When we arrived at Broadway Methodist, we were taken to the second floor where the Intensive Care Unit was located. We were ushered into the waiting room where Mom and the rest of the family were waiting. They updated us on Dad's condition. He had a fairly good night, though he was in horrible pain. An

The Final Service

angiogram needed to be done, but the doctors could not because of the infection in his lungs. The next ICU visiting hour would be soon, and Mom told us we could go see him then.

After we had been there for a few minutes, we met the head of the nursing staff. Many years ago she had heard Dad preach, and her life had been affected by the ministry of Jack Hyles. We were blessed to have people caring for Dad who already loved and appreciated him.

At first the hospital staff was a little bit leery of all the attention being paid to Dad. Brother Clyde Wolfe and his Hyles-Anderson College security staff had stationed themselves at the hospital so that no one could get to my dad or the family. A security guard was in the lobby at all times, and another one remained in the general waiting room outside the ICU. These men proved to be more than just guards; they proved to be incredible servants.

The entire time that Dad was in the hospital, these dear men were there to serve us at their own expense. They came, and they stayed with us in the background the entire time Dad was in the hospital. They got coffee for us, brought newspapers to us, made phone calls for us, and looked for ways they could be of help. There is no way to describe the comfort they brought to Mom and the family, just knowing they were looking out for us.

To some it may have seemed a little cold to have men standing guard, but with all of the thousands of church members who knew Dad, it could have been a real problem if they had begun to come to the hospital to try to find out some information. I was so grateful that these men were there to help us; and on behalf of my family, I want to say a special thanks to them.

The Passing Over of Dr. Jack Hyles

After a few minutes, it was finally visiting time. Broadway Methodist had four half-hours a day that we could visit a patient in the ICU. During these times, two at a time could go into the room. Since we had just arrived, Mom took my wife Brenda and me to the room to see Dad. To be honest, Dad did not know how sick he was at this point; at least we did not think he did. We were afraid of scaring him. I was very concerned when I walked into the room that he would think the family had been called because he was dying; and it might make matters worse. Dad knew he was sick, but I am sure he was not yet fully aware of how critical his condition was.

Actually, I am not sure any of the family members really knew Dad's condition. Truthfully, it was very difficult to understand the severity of the situation. To us, Dad was and had always been invulnerable. In our minds, it was hard to fathom that a man who had been so vibrant just days and weeks before could be this sick. I had just seen him a few weeks previously, and he seemed so healthy and so alive. The truth is Dad was very sick. In fact, he was dying. Had he stayed at home and sat in that chair long enough, he would have died in that chair. He was that ill.

When I was taken into Dad's room, I was afraid of my own emotions. My first words were, "If you think you are going into the hospital, and I am not coming to see you, you are crazy." Dad smiled and said, "Good to see you, Doc." Brenda and I went to his bedside, and Dad began to tell us about his experience in Monterey. Somehow he had inside knowledge that Monterey was the end. He told everybody the Monterey story when they first came to see him; and every time he would tell it, he would get very emotional. Tears would well up in his eyes. We chatted

The Final Service

for a little while, but Dad was fighting to show some strength to us, so we could not tell just how sick he was except for what the medical staff was telling us.

Throughout that first day in the hospital, the doctors told us, "Your dad is not strong enough to go through an angiogram, but we need to put him through one to find out exactly the extent of the problem. He is not strong enough because of the infection in his lungs. We are afraid the tests present too big of a risk." We began to hear such terms as "high-risk patient," so we knew he was in serious condition, but we still did not realize how serious his heart condition was.

The doctors ran a number of tests and put Dad on several antibiotics trying to defeat the infection. A blood culture was taken for tuberculosis, with the thought of the possibility of his having contracted that while he was in Mexico. The doctors tried to do everything they could to get him into the condition where an angiogram could be performed to see how serious his condition was.

The one detail that surprised us all was that Dad asked few questions about the church work. I think that he knew that it might be over, and it appeared to me that he was just going to let things go for now and allow them to run their course. We were all glad and somewhat relieved that Dad was not trying to pastor the church from his hospital bed. We knew that it was not good for his health, and we knew that he needed to be more concerned about himself and not to worry about church business. Throughout that first day, we would go and see him during each visiting time. Each of us wanted just to have a few minutes with him, but we all gave Mom the right to have most of the time with him. He finally seemed to stabilize, but the doctors

The Passing Over of Dr. Jack Hyles

remained concerned about the need to perform the angiogram. Answers to questions about the exact state of his health were needed.

Later that day, Jon and Teresa Horton, my oldest sister Becky's daughter and son-in-law, arrived from Arkansas. Jon is a young pastor of a new church, and they had driven to Hammond upon hearing news of Dad's condition. Jon and Teresa had graduated from Hyles-Anderson College, and the previous summer Mom and Dad had given them a beautiful going away shower at their condominium. It had been a wonderful evening and, I am certain, a memorable experience for this sweet young couple. Their arrival would prove to be a blessing in numerous ways. Not only was it good for Dad to get to see his granddaughter, but they were incredibly helpful throughout the ordeal. Jon is a fine, unassuming young man who had not tried to cash in on the fame of his grandfather-in-law. Instead, he was (and is) a humble servant who was willing to do any task for the family while Dad was in the hospital. Both of them were precious to have with us.

That Wednesday evening was one of the graduation services for Hyles-Anderson College. Obviously, Dad could not be there. Brenda and I stayed with Mom at the hospital during church. It was getting late, and we encouraged Mom to go home and get some rest. Rest would become a very important part of seeing us through these next few days even though we did not know what we were up against at this point. After the final visiting hour, Mom did go home to rest. I sent my wife Brenda and our daughters to the hotel to sleep. I sat up with Dad throughout the night.

That night at First Baptist Church, the news was announced

The Final Service

about Dad's heart attack. The people were concerned, but like us they did not know the true extent of their preacher's illness. At this point, let me on behalf of the family say how grateful we were to all the people of First Baptist Church for their graciousness and kindness during this time. The people respected our privacy, and yet we know their prayers and their hearts were extended to Dad during this time. We wanted to keep them informed as much as we could, but we truly did not know any more to share. Little did we or his church people know that when Dad walked out of his pulpit on Wednesday night, January 24, he would never return.

CHAPTER

3

An Emergency Procedure

"What time I am afraid, I will trust in thee."
(Psalms 56:3)

Y SECOND DAY IN Indiana proved to be a very eventful day in the final days of my dad's life. I had decided to stay all night Wednesday so that someone from the family would be with Dad. Though I sat in the chair most of the night, I paced in the waiting room and many times walked down the hallway to ICU just to look in on Dad while he slept. He seemed to have a decent night of rest though he was still racked with back pain.

I was tired; it was my second night without sleep. About 9:00 that morning, my sister Cindy arrived at the hospital. Soon after, Mom came. We went down to his room for a good visit during one of the full visiting half hours we were allowed. I went to the hotel room and finally got a long overdo shower and freshened up before going back to the hospital for what would

An Emergency Procedure

prove to be a very, very busy and special day.

Dad seemed to be stable. The doctor had told us that it was not safe to do the angiogram until his lungs cleared up from the infection. As I mentioned before, he had been tested for tuberculosis, but the results would not be conclusive for 20 days. Dad's recent trip to Mexico caused them to think that it was a possibility but not a probability. In the meantime, antibiotics were administered as heavily as possible in order to clear up the infection, but the high dosages did not seem to be doing any good.

Around noon that day, they called Mom to Dad's room. Something seemed wrong. We discovered that Dad's blood pressure was dropping rapidly, and concern arose about losing him. A decision was made to do the angiogram. When we heard this news, we were gripped with fear. Each of us made the walk to his room to spend a few minutes with him. For his sake, we did not want to appear to be panicking. We all just wanted to see him as much as possible before he went in for this critical procedure.

Brother Colsten did what he does so well; he went to Dad's room and prayed with him before Dad went for the angiogram. To say that we were all fearful and somewhat anticipating the worst is an understatement. We walked with him to the area where they would perform the angiogram. The entire family accompanied him on that walk. As always, Dad's spirits seemed good and strong. He seemed to be the encourager instead of the one who needed the encouragement, but I could definitely see a fear in his eyes. When we finally reached the area, our family went to the waiting room. Mom, Cindy, and I walked into the location where they would do the angiogram. Mom and Cindy

The Passing Over of Dr. Jack Hyles

both kissed him and told him they loved him. I remember bending down, kissing him on the forehead, and telling him I loved him, too, but Dad, with his typical humor, looked up when I kissed him and said, "Yuck." We chuckled, but honestly a part of me feared that I was saying goodbye to him. I remember the horrible feeling when they wheeled him away from us, and we wondered if this moment was it.

Back in the waiting room, the assistant pastors of the church had gathered with the family, and we all waited, hoping the procedure would go well. A prayer meeting broke out, and several of the men voiced prayers out loud for the success of this procedure. A while later, the doctor came in and said that the angiogram was completed and that Dad had come through it very, very well. He explained that while the angiogram was being performed, they took advantage of the opportunity to insert a balloon pump into his heart that would help with the pumping of the heart and make it stronger. With the good news came the bad; the doctors discovered several arteries were 90 percent closed. They also discovered that his heart was only operating at about 20 percent of its capacity. They learned that open heart surgery would have to be performed in order for Dad to even live. However, the doctors felt they were not able to perform surgery at Broadway Methodist Hospital because he was such a high-risk patient. For those reasons, the doctors asked permission to airlift him to the University of Chicago Hospitals to receive the care that he so desperately needed.

We were relieved to know that there was hope, yet we were also so very concerned. Dad would now have to go to another hospital and have very serious surgery. The doctors also indicated to us that it was possible that as soon as he landed,

An Emergency Procedure

surgery would be performed. It appeared that this surgery was very, very critical. God intervened, and through a series of events, the surgery did not take place on Thursday or Friday, but on the following Monday. That delay allowed us to spend time alone with Dad and also allowed more family members to arrive and see him before he passed away.

We waited for several hours to hear the word that Dad would be airlifted, but the doctors continued to work on him. He continued to have problems with the lung infection. In fact, several times the team of doctors became alarmed at his condition. They worked feverishly on him trying to prepare him for this move. We also faced the problem of no bed being available at the other hospital, and we had to wait for one to become available.

The moments turned into hours, and we sat until after midnight, waiting for word that he was leaving. We wanted to be at the hospital, waiting for him when he arrived. Finally, a doctor said, "We are getting ready to take him; you should leave." Jack and I drove Mom to the University of Chicago Hospitals where we would begin the final days of vigil.

Jack and I decided to drive Mom to the Chicago hospital while Jon Horton stayed with Dad, so that there was still a family member present. The security guards were stationed at both hospitals. Once again, I cannot begin to tell what a blessing these men were. Clyde Wolfe literally stayed with my dad until he was on the helicopter. Two other men waited with the family at the University of Chicago Hospitals, having made arrangements for our arrival. They even parked the car for us when we arrived there.

As soon as the helicopter took off, we were contacted and

The Passing Over of Dr. Jack Hyles

told that Dad was on his way. Sometime around 1:30 A.M., he arrived at his new location. We were anticipating the possibility that they would be taking him into surgery immediately, but it became apparent that the surgery would wait at least for a day.

One interesting story about Dad's airlifting concerns a nurse named Kim. She stayed by my dad's side and worked with him as they prepared him to be airlifted. She stayed past her shift and continued to meet any need he had. This young nurse was an incredible blessing to Dad, and it did not slip by his notice. As he was being put on the helicopter, he began to ask, "What is the name of that nurse? I want her name. Somebody get me her name." We soon learned her name was Kim Shoemaker. Why was he so desperately trying to find her name? As always, Dad wanted to let her know he was grateful. He probably would have put her name on a 3x5 card and made a little note to send her a short letter or maybe a small token of appreciation, and then he would have put it in his shirt pocket. For you see, you couldn't do something for Dad and have it escape his notice. Gratitude was his way of life. Anyone who was good to him deserved and received his thanks. This was one of those things about his life that was so amazing to me. I am grateful to those security guards who made every effort to get her name. By the way, Kim Shoemaker did receive a letter—not from Jack Hyles—but from a grateful son on behalf of his father.

The move to the University of Chicago Hospitals was very disconcerting and quite a difficult move for Dad. It was very interesting how hard it was for him to get accustomed to this idea; he wanted to stay at Broadway Methodist because of Dr. Streeter. He did not want to be airlifted to some place where a stranger would do surgery on him. He requested that Dr. Henry

An Emergency Procedure

Giragos, a heart specialist who is a member of the First Baptist Church, do the surgery, but he did not specialize in the kind of surgery Dad needed; and he strongly recommended against it. Dad did not understand that he was in a very, very critical condition, and the doctor who would perform surgery on him was one of the top surgeons in the nation for this type of surgery.

We knew Dad needed at least three bypasses and one valve replacement, and the attending doctors knew his heart was very, very weak. They also knew that no local hospital could give him the care he needed and that the University of Chicago Hospitals was his only hope. He could not understand that fact nor could we, but he reluctantly accepted the decision only after Dr. Streeter and Dr. Giragos assured him that this move was best for him.

It was also difficult for Dad because he did not feel loved by the people there. At Broadway Methodist Hospital in Merrillville, people knew who he was. He felt a different kind of a spirit of love from those people. He felt at home. He knew Dr. Streeter was nearby, and he knew the whole family was close at hand. He struggled with this feeling, and he even said at one time, "They do not love me here." He was soon to find out how wrong he was because everywhere Jack Hyles went, he loved people; and they soon learned to love him as well.

The hospital where Dad was taken was also a university hospital. On the first day of Dad's stay there, he was inundated by students, or as we called them—doctor wannabe's. The students would come into his room and grill him with repetitious questions, many of which seemed to be so ridiculous and useless. Dad seldom tolerated stupidity, and it was very difficult for him to lie there in that bed while some young college students asked

The Passing Over of Dr. Jack Hyles

him questions about his medical past.

At one point, I teased him a little about it and said, "Dad, why in the world are you being so nice to these people who are asking you dumb questions?" (Anyone who has been in a Question-and-Answer Hour with my dad knows that asking a dumb question is a silly thing to do.) At times, a group of student doctors would stand around his bed, asking him questions. What a perfect opportunity for the real Jack Hyles to put them in their place, but he never did. His reasoning was simple as he explained with a sparkle in his eyes, "They may determine whether I live or die."

The first day at this hospital, Dad got very little rest. People were around him constantly. The pain in his back was much worse because he could no longer turn over or sit up since the balloon had been put in his heart. Until the surgery, he had to lie on his back constantly. At times, sitting up had given him some relief. In fact, for a couple of weeks the only way he had gotten any sleep was by sitting up in a chair. By now, the pain in his back was even more excruciating.

Sometimes when the pain became so extreme, Dad would call two of us into his room. He would ask us to take him by the arms and just try to prop him up a little bit more and position the pillows in a different way that would give him some relief. It was difficult to see Dad suffering so terribly, and I am sure the pain was even greater than we had realized. We had never known him to complain, but it was obvious that the pain was terrible.

One blessing at the University of Chicago Hospitals was that they allowed him to have his Diet Dr. Pepper, and we kept him in good supply. This seemed to be refreshing to Dad.

An Emergency Procedure

Shortly after our arrival, the resident doctor, Dr. David Jayakar, who would be in charge of Dad's case as well as perform the surgery, came to meet with us. He was Indian; and upon meeting him, we wondered what kind of man he would be. Dr. Jayakar turned out to be a real gentleman, who took a great deal of time to explain every detail. Two statements he made caught our attention. First he said, "I am here to serve you." And secondly he talked about his faith in God. Something inside of our spirits was knit with this man. Could it be that the Holy Spirit was bearing witness between his spirit and ours that he was a child of God? He did have a Christian name—David. We later learned that he was born again. When Dr. Jayakar shared his faith with my dad, it gave Dad tremendous peace and confidence that a fellow believer would be performing his surgery.

The fact that Dr. Jayakar was a servant touched our hearts. We knew that the one upon whom he would be performing surgery also had a servant's heart and that was why he was so successful in his chosen field. Yet, here was one of the greatest doctors in the world in his field who also saw himself as nothing more than a servant. Dr. Jayakar was truly a servant. Through Dad's entire stay, he was always so careful to meet the needs we had and to carefully and meticulously answer any questions. We were thrilled to know that he was a Christian. Dad also liked the fact that Dr. Jayakar lived in his hometown of Munster, Indiana.

When Dr. Jayakar spoke to us about Dad's condition, he carefully explained that Dad was in critical condition, but stable. The surgeons didn't want to operate until Monday when hopefully Dad's heart would be stronger. He explained in more detail what the doctors at Broadway Methodist Hospital had told

The Passing Over of Dr. Jack Hyles

us about Dad's heart being damaged, and that he had had experienced more than one heart attack.

The nurses at Broadway Methodist had treated my dad with tremendous care. It was apparent that they loved him. They knew who he was, and they wanted to do everything they could to make him comfortable. One of the great early blessings at the University of Chicago Hospitals came in the person of a young man named John. I walked into Dad's room, and the attending nurse was a nice-looking, athletically built young man. He introduced himself with a handshake and said, "My name is John." Dad said, "John lives in St. John." After talking with him further, we learned that he lived only a block away from Eddie Lapina, one of Dad's assistant pastors.

John was a cheerful young man. He shared how he had gone to school to become an accountant but found no passion in the job for him. He quit his job and went back to school to become a nurse. He loved helping people. An almost instant bond formed between John and Dad, as you will see later in this book. John was a people person and a talker, and he and Dad would talk and tease. John did not treat Dad like a sick old man; he treated him like a friend and cared for him with great concern. I believe we can say that John treated Dad with the dignity and respect that he deserved. For that honor, we are grateful to this fine young nurse.

By the end of the day on Friday, we were all exhausted. None of us had slept much since Monday night. The past 24 hours had been grueling to all of us; but most of all, we were concerned about Dad. He had really suffered, and we were all concerned about what he was still facing. Mom was weary, and Dad was concerned about her health; so we decided to take her

An Emergency Procedure

home and let her get a decent night of rest. That was also my first night of sleep since Monday night. It was difficult for Mom and Dad to be separated during this uneasy time, but Mom knew Dad would worry even more; so she did what was best for him as well as for herself. Jack slept some during the day on Friday and returned to keep the night shift vigil.

Waiting until Monday for Dad to have surgery in some ways brought great fear and in other ways great blessing. The wait would cause Dad to suffer a lot more pain, but in retrospect, we were given several more days to spend a few last moments with our beloved. During this time, other members of the family were also able to get into town and spend some time with Dad.

Friday night I was exhausted, but I struggled with the thought of leaving Dad alone. I could hardly stand being away from him. I am sure everyone in the family felt the same way. All of us had sat vigil with him throughout this day. We had encouraged Mom to try to sleep as much as possible. Dad worried so much about her. It was interesting. Dad wanted Mom with him and would ask constantly if she was there; but he would also push her to go home to get some rest. I took it upon myself to be the decision-maker for Mom throughout these last days. I would tell Dad that I was taking Mom home, though she did not want to, and it was true, so that she could get rest. Dad would always say, "Good, Son. Thank you, Mom needs to get some sleep. I am worried about her." Oh, how he loved her; and oh, how he lived to meet her every need. That desire never changed the entire time he was in the hospital. I was fatigued; we all were. For the first time since Sunday night, I went back to get a night's sleep.

On Saturday, Becky, my oldest sister, and her husband Tim

The Passing Over of Dr. Jack Hyles

were able to come and spend some precious moments with Dad. Their daughter Trina and her husband, Steve Beebe, were also able to come. I happened to be in the room for one very sweet moment. Dad looked at his oldest granddaughter, now a mother of two, and said, "Trina, you know, when I get out of here, if God lets me live, I am not going to be able to do what I have been doing. My ministry is probably over, so when I get out of here, I am going to take you to the zoo; and if there is a kiddie park nearby, you and I are going to go to the kiddie park." He smiled with that "patented Jack-Hyles grin."

Trina looked warmly at him and replied, "Good, Grandpa. I will get a babysitter for my kids so that you and I can go." What a sweet and precious moment that was. Dad was so delighted to see each member of the family, and though he was in terrible pain and struggling for breath, they were sweet moments for him. He savored the presence and company of those who loved him.

In some ways, the weekend was uneventful. However, that Saturday and Sunday proved to be two of the most important of Dad's final days. He found it difficult to wait for surgery, and his pain was excruciating; but during these final two days we individually were able to spend the most quality time with him. Mom would go into his room for long, long periods of time and just stand and talk to him. They enjoyed each other's company so much and for so long. Their time together almost seemed too sacred for us to violate. So many times, we would just stay in the waiting area and allow Mom to have the time she needed and wanted.

All day Saturday we sat and waited throughout the day at the hospital. We had the opportunity of coming and going and

An Emergency Procedure

spending moments here and there with Dad. He slept as much as possible, but we also spent as much of his waking time with him as we could. Each member of the family spent some time with him as we sat and waited for surgery to come. That Saturday night, my wife and I stayed all night with Dad.

We tried to sleep. Broadway Methodist had recliners and couches, but one distinct memory I have about the University of Chicago Hospitals is that it was not a comfortable place to wait. The waiting rooms have the most uncomfortable chairs, and there is no place to stretch out and sleep. With the help of the security guards, we did our best to try to sleep between our visits. They woke me up every hour, and I would walk to Dad's unit just to look in on him. That night, before he was trying to go to sleep, he said, "Son, just look in on me every once in a while and see how I am doing. If I am awake, come on in and talk to me for a while."

Brenda and I tried to get some rest. The security guards who stayed faithfully at their posts did as I requested and would wake me up on the hour so that I could check on Dad. From ten o'clock until midnight, he had suffered the severest pain of the entire time he had been sick. At one point, he even said, "I would almost rather die than have to experience this pain. It is almost beyond what I can bear."

At two o'clock in the morning, the security guard woke me again. This time when I went to Dad's room, I stood by his bed for two hours while he slept; and I relived a lifetime of experiences. In my mind, I went to ball games that we had gone to when I was a little boy. I relived playing catch in the backyard and shooting baskets at the basketball hoop above the garage. I relived the night in 1959 when I went with my dad on a Saturday

The Passing Over of Dr. Jack Hyles

night as he preached at the Union Gospel Rescue Mission in Hammond, Indiana. I remembered how later that night I got out of bed and went down to the living room to tell my grandmother that I wanted to be saved. My mother was in the hospital having given birth to my youngest sister, Cindy. When Dad came home that night, he led me to Christ. I relived our family devotions. I relived dinnertime with the family all around the table. I relived a thousand experiences with this good man, my dad. I spent two hours just thanking God for my father.

I left to lie down for another hour. When one of the security guards again woke me, it was about five o'clock. This time when I went to his room, Dad was awake. For the next two hours, I got to spend time with my dad talking and just sharing. He was still in pain, and he was very tired. His breathing was very labored, and occasionally he would close his eyes and doze off for a couple of minutes. When he would awaken, we would just chat. I do not know that we said anything really profound; but, father and son, we just talked as I stood next to his bed early that Sunday morning.

As usual, Dad asked me, "Son, who stayed guard last night?" I answered, "Clyde Wolfe, Lee Comstock, Dave Sisson, and Dale Breed."

"Those are all good and loyal men, Dave," he commented. "I never demanded or even asked for that kind of loyalty; they just gave it to me." I think that what Dad was trying to say was that some people could not understand that the loyalty people had for him was not a loyalty of tyranny; it was a loyalty of love. Theirs was not loyalty to a dictator but loyalty to a servant. I understood, and I think all who knew Dad well realized the loyalty he was given was out of loyalty to someone who had

An Emergency Procedure

served them well.

Another time Dad said to me, "Son, it is funny the things that I now want that I never thought that I would want. I wanted a big fiftieth wedding anniversary celebration for your mom's sake. I wanted a big fortieth anniversary celebration as pastor of First Baptist Church, and the people were so kind in making that a special event with the banquet. I also wanted someone from the family to be here with me every moment that I have been in the hospital." When he made that last statement, my heart was warmed; I was so glad that we had stayed with him.

Shortly thereafter, breakfast arrived; and the nursing staff arrived to do a little work on Dad, so I was asked to step out of his room. I will never forget what Dad said to me just before I left. He took my hand, and he said, "Son, thanks for staying with me last night. You will never know how much I appreciate it. You helped me make it through the night." I left, with tears in my eyes, glad to have had a wonderful night—the last night that I would ever spend with my dad.

I am so thankful that in the last years of Dad's life, we had become close and had spent as much time as possible together. Dad would ask me advice about things in the church and ministries. We would talk about the condition of fundamental, independent Baptists across America. Once when we were together, we even dreamed up the 2001 Pastors' School theme that would be held in March. Together we came up with the theme, "The Miracle of Miller Road," and just a few weeks before, he had asked me to help him to decide on what subjects he should teach. Dad had begun including me in many of his ideas for his ministry and confided in me regarding many aspects of the future plans he had made.

The Passing Over of Dr. Jack Hyles

Sunday morning was a beautiful, sunshiny day. Mom arrived at the hospital early. It would prove to be a very tense day at First Baptist Church of Hammond. It would be a day of anticipation for a church wondering what the future held for their beloved pastor.

Dr. Wendell Evans, President of Hyles-Anderson College and Dad's dear friend of many years, preached in place of Dad that Sunday morning at First Baptist Church. He had been scheduled to be at my home church, Pinellas Park Baptist Temple, for a missions conference. Brother Farris, my pastor, called and said, "Let Dr. Evans know that if he is needed there, please, do not hesitate to cancel." I knew this would be the third time a prominent speaker had canceled on Brother Farris in the past six months. Dr. Bob Gray had become very ill and had to cancel speaking at our Sunday school convention in September. In December, Dad and Mom were to be there, and a blizzard in Chicago prevented their coming. The Chicago airports were closed, and Dad had to cancel that Monday meeting. Now, Brother Farris was facing another cancellation, but he did so graciously because he wanted to do what was best for First Baptist Church and Hyles-Anderson College. Dr. Evans preached a marvelous, encouraging message to the church people that morning.

When Mom arrived at the hospital, Brenda and I were very weary from being up all night. We drove back to Indiana to rest, shower, and freshen up a little bit. We were back at the hospital shortly after noon. When we arrived, Cindy and her family, along with my two girls, had come from church. We all had lunch together, and each of us spent some individual time with Dad. He had had a rough night, but he still managed to get some

An Emergency Procedure

rest that he desperately needed. On this day, he would spend more time with Mom than any previous day of his illness.

Sunday came and went without much incident, but it was not an insignificant day to us. In fact, it was a precious jewel in the memory of all of us who would soon say goodbye to him for the final time—until we see him again in Heaven.

4

The Day of Surgery

*"Yea, though I walk through the valley of the shadow of death,
I will fear no evil: for thou art with me;
thy rod and thy staff they comfort me."*
(Psalms 23:4)

ONDAY MORNING, FEBRUARY 5, 2001, at 5:00, we picked up Mom at her condominium. We had anticipated this day; Dad would be in surgery most of the day. We prepared ourselves for what we thought would be a very, very, long, tiring time that would undoubtedly drag through the night and into the next day. Although we did not know exactly all we would face, we knew that it would undoubtedly be very tense and difficult.

As we drove to the University of Chicago Hospital that morning, Mom seemed fearful yet confident that everything was going to be okay. There was still in all of us a lack of true understanding of the extent of how ill Dad was. As much as we

The Day of Surgery

tried to understand it, it was simply impossible for us to realize the severity of his condition. Upon arriving at the hospital, we parked in the garage, checked into the front, and then made our way up to the fifth floor where Dad was being kept in the intensive care ward.

Seemingly, Dad had a fairly good night of rest. He was very calm and at peace facing this major surgery. I went into his room first and chatted with him for just a couple of minutes. After a few minutes, Mom joined us; I gave them a little time to be alone. Within the next 30 minutes, the family began to arrive. My older sister Becky and her husband Tim and their children, Trina with her husband Steve and Teresa with her husband Jon came. My daughters, Amy and Bethany, were with us. Jack and Cindy and their children, Jaclynn and Kenny walked into the waiting room. Then my aunt, Dad's sister and only living sibling Earlyne, came.

Finally, it became apparent that it was time for Dad to get ready. He called for all of us to come down and see him. We walked to his room in the Intensive Care and gathered around his bed to say goodbye to him before his surgery. It was early in the morning, so John, his buddy and nurse, was on duty. He was grateful that John was there with him. As we gathered around his bed, he was obviously in very good spirits, but his eyes revealed a sense of anticipation and apprehension.

I remember one thing very specifically about this last gathering. One by one, Dad took the hand of each of us, looked us in the eyes, and said, "I love you." He was not morbid nor was he terribly emotional, but he was very, very serious. We stood around his bed and chatted, cut up a little, as it always was when the Hyles clan were together. Finally, Dad looked at us as a

The Passing Over of Dr. Jack Hyles

group and said, "You are all great. I am proud of you all. I love you. Now get out of here before I start to cry." We all chuckled a little bit, and then we turned, and one by one, we walked out of the room. I lingered for a little while behind the others. After everyone had left, I went back into his room and said, "Dad, when you get out of here, can we go to a ball game or two? It has been a lot of years since we have done that." He smiled and said, "Sure, Son." I shook his hand again and said, "I love you."

"I love you, too, Son." I left his room.

Mom stayed with him for a few minutes until he was taken away for surgery. Of course, none of us knew until later that these sweet moments would be the last time we would see him conscious. Mom worried later about whether or not she had properly said goodbye to him, and we were able to assure her that she had.

As Dad was being rolled to surgery, John, his nurse, accompanied him. As they came to the door to go in for surgery where the anesthesiologists were waiting, Dad reached up and grabbed the back of John's head and neck, pulled him down to himself, and said, "Thank you for all you have done for me. I love you, John."

And John said, "I love you, too." Then John turned to us and said, "He is scared," and then he said, "This is a good man."

Dad was taken into surgery. None of us knew that within minutes Dad would suffer another heart attack that would eventually prove to be one of the major causes of his death.

The surgery waiting room on the same floor where Dad was having surgery was a little crowded. Since there were so many of us, we decided to go back to the fifth floor where we had been waiting throughout our vigil with Dad. When we arrived

The Day of Surgery

upstairs, Brother Eddie Lapina, his wife Jamie, and Brother Jeff Owens and his wife Schery, had arrived with boxes and baskets of snacks and drinks for our family to enjoy while we waited. Brother Ray Young also waited in the lobby during the surgery.

The almost eerie atmosphere was filled with understandable tension, but also lots of laughter and playfulness. I believe that is how Dad would have wanted the wait to be. Even at the worst of times, he had always kept his wit and humor. Little did we know that the fight for Dad's life was raging in a surgery room not too far from where we were waiting for him. We had so much hope because we knew that thousands and maybe even tens of thousands of people all over the world were praying for him while he was in surgery.

Afternoon came, and we still had not heard any word. We were asked to wait in a different location, because the area where we were waiting was used every week at that time for a meeting with transplant patients, people who were candidates for heart transplants. We gathered our things and began to try to filter throughout the hospital. The First Baptist Church staff men who were there with their families waited in the main lobby. We returned to the surgical waiting room and found it had emptied quite a bit from the early day surgeries, which were already finished. The more time that passed, the more fear and apprehension we were feeling. We tried to busy ourselves. We had been told the surgery would last somewhere between five and seven hours. As far as we knew, he had gone into surgery around nine o'clock, so we anticipated hearing something around four o'clock. Four o'clock came and went, and there was still no word.

Mom had left for a few minutes to take a break when the

The Passing Over of Dr. Jack Hyles

phone rang in the surgical waiting room around 5:30. Someone picked up the phone, listened and asked, "Mrs. Hyles?"

I jumped up, ran, and said, "She is not in here right now, but I am Mr. Hyles' son." The person handed me the phone. A nurse on the other end said, "Mr. Hyles, your father is still in surgery. We had some complications. We had to do several bypasses, but when we went in to replace the valve, we found that there was another valve not working. We must do a second valve replacement. He will probably be in surgery for another hour and a half."

I quickly asked, "Is he doing well?"

"You have to understand, this is a very delicate part of the surgery, and he was already in very critical condition," she said. "Still, I think everything is going as well as can be expected."

Somehow I sensed in her voice that everything was not so good. I felt a stab of fear go through me. I did not want to alarm my mom, so I only related the facts to her. Yet down deep inside, I feared the surgery was not going as well as we had hoped. Thankfully, Dr. Dennis Streeter came into the surgery waiting area to carefully explain in layman's terms about the valve replacements and the surgery itself. He was a great help to us in understanding what was happening with Dad.

All of us were obviously overwhelmed because we realized at this moment that there was even more to Dad's surgery than what we had thought at the beginning. The next hour and a half were some of the most anxious moments. It is amazing to sit and watch other families waiting for someone to come and tell them about their loved ones while doing the same. We saw others receive good news, pack their belongings, and leave to see their loved one. Most everyone had cleared out of the waiting room

The Day of Surgery

while we were still waiting for some word.

True to their projection, almost an hour and a half later, the phone rang and again I heard, "Mrs. Hyles?" She took the phone. The doctor explained to her that the surgery was now over. He shared the incredible news that Dad had suffered another heart attack at the beginning of his surgery, and that emergency surgery had to be performed on him as a result. The news sounded very grim. "To protect your husband, we are going to leave him in the surgery room to recover for about another hour and a half before we move him upstairs to ICU."

The surgery waiting room was closing, so we returned to the ICU waiting room to again wait for Dad to be brought back to his room. About 8:30, a nurse finally came and reported, "He is back in his room. The doctor will be out shortly to talk with your family." The conversation with the doctor would be the most eye-opening moment that we had yet experienced during the entire ordeal.

5

His Final Hours

*"But he, being full of the Holy Ghost, looked up stedfastly
into heaven, and saw the glory of God,
and Jesus standing on the right hand of God,
And said, Behold, I see the heavens opened,
and the Son of man standing on the right hand of God."*
(Acts 7:55-56)

R. JAYAKAR ENTERED THE waiting room at about 8:40 Monday night. For approximately 12 hours, he had labored diligently to help give Dad an opportunity to live. I could see he was weary and worn from the long day of surgery. He sat down across from us, and with the same meek, gentle spirit, he began to explain to us all that had happened during the day.

He began by explaining to us that Dad's was a very delicate, difficult, and high-risk surgery that he would not have ordinarily performed on anyone. He said that he chose to do it because of

His Final Hours

Dad's spirit and his love of life. He felt that if anyone could survive such a surgery, it would be him. Those carefully chosen words made me begin to realize perhaps for the first time the severity of Dad's illness.

We learned that shortly after Dad had gone into the operating room, while the anesthesia was being administered, he had suffered a massive heart attack. Fortunately, the doctors were all ready, so they were able to immediately open his chest wall and begin heart massage. The surgery team immediately went to work trying to repair the additional damage. The team performed three bypasses and then found that not only was the original valve damaged, but another main valve had stopped working completely. They replaced that valve as well. While they were in surgery, the inside walls of the heart began to hemorrhage, adding even more complications to the surgery. Step-by-step, the doctor described the difficult and grueling work that had been performed on Dad's heart. He then began to share what we were facing.

He explained that Dad was being kept paralyzed and in a coma to keep him from waking up. He had to overcome three major hurdles in order to survive the surgery. The first hurdle was to get through the night and to get his breathing stabilized. His lungs were still full of fluid; but if he could be stabilized, the doctors felt he would have overcome the first.

The second hurdle would be bringing him out of the coma and waking him. With this procedure came possibilities of another heart attack or perhaps even more hemorrhaging. The situation would be touch and go when the doctors attempted to revive him.

Finally, the third hurdle would be to see if his heart was

The Passing Over of Dr. Jack Hyles

strong enough to begin beating on its own. We knew his heart was severely damaged, but exactly how extensively it was damaged was yet unknown. There was fear that the damage could be bad enough that the heart muscle would not be strong enough to sustain his life.

Mom asked Dr. Jayakar, "How long until he is out of the woods?"

His answer startled us. "At least seven days before we know that he can make it."

We were all stunned. Perhaps for the first time, we really understood how ill Dad was. In reality, he had been dying, and we did not know. We still had hope, but our hope was greatly tempered. Now, the realization that we just might lose him had begun to sink in. I still vividly remember the eerie silence that permeated the waiting room as we pondered what we faced.

Dr. Jayakar recommended that we all go home and try to sleep. He told us that if Dad made it through the night and into the next day, he would need us there by his side when they awakened him. Dr. Jayakar felt it was critical for us to be rested in order to be the best possible help to Dad. We were faced with a tough decision; not one moment had passed since Dad entered the hospital that a family member had not been with him. Still, our doctor seemed sure that this was the right decision. Finally, we agreed to take his advice and go home to sleep, and as a family, we agreed at what time we would assemble the next day. We were promised that if anything happened we would be called during the night. One of the security guards was asked to remain in the family waiting room. I gave him my phone number and "left final instructions," to make certain I was called if anything happened during the night.

His Final Hours

For some strange reason, none of us wanted to go into Dad's room. I now believe we were all afraid of how Dad would look. I know I was afraid for Mom to see him after surgery. I had seen people come out from open-heart surgery before; and I knew how terrible they could look. I was terribly afraid for Mom.

Just as we were leaving, for some strange reason, I was drawn back toward his room, so I stepped in and looked at Dad. There he was hanging between life and death while doctors and nurses attended him, trying to keep him alive. Jack also walked back into the room with me. Dr. Jayakar took us into a little room next to Dad's and said, "Let me show you what is happening in his lungs." He showed us what a healthy set of lungs should look like, and then he showed us a picture of Dad's lungs. Then he explained, "This is what we are fighting right now." Sure enough, we could see that the infection and the congestion in his lungs were incredible. Then Dr. Jayakar added, "Right now, we are just tying to help keep him breathing." I guess after seeing the x-rays, I was more aware than ever that Dad's chances of survival were not very good. I cannot say that I lost hope, but I can say that I began to feel that the chances of our losing him were greater than keeping him.

We finally got everyone into the cars, and we headed back home to try to sleep as much as we could. Some of us couldn't help but wonder if we would ever see Dad alive again.

By the time we dropped off Mom at her condominium and got back to the motel where we were staying, it was about 10:00. Brenda and I were both emotionally and physically exhausted. Ours had been an incredible ordeal. My heart was filled with fear and foreboding, yet I know I also felt hope. Somehow I had this feeling that Dad was going to make it; I wanted to believe that

The Passing Over of Dr. Jack Hyles

he would. I had a deep hope that almost turned into expectation. I also felt that Dad was not ready to die. After all, he had too many reasons to live. By the time we had laid down to sleep, the hour was very late. My mind was filled with mixed emotions, and I didn't think I could possibly sleep.

The phone rang awakening me. I remembered I had given my number to the security guard in the waiting room in case Dad's condition changed. I looked at the clock; it was 12:30, Tuesday morning. I knew something was wrong. I answered the phone, and the security guard said, "Brother Hyles, you told me to call. The attending doctor is here and asked to speak to you." I waited and then heard her say, "Mr. Hyles, your father has taken a turn for the worse. I feel it would be advisable for the family to come back. I believe some decisions will have to be made."

"Yes, Ma'am, thank you." I said. "I will be there in a few minutes."

I hung up the phone not knowing what to do. Dad's surgeon had advised, "Go home and get some rest. Your Dad will need you later in the day." Now, our intern doctor (whose name was Judith) said to come back now. I called Jack and told him what had happened. We agreed that there was only one person who could make that decision, and that was Mom. I dialed Mom's number. When she answered, barely awake, and obviously very weary, I said, "Mom, the hospital called, and they want us to come back. Dad has taken a turn for the worse."

My Mom's reply amazed me. She said, "David, God told me that Dad was going to die on February 6, and something was going to happen around midnight. Last night I gave Dad to the Lord."

His Final Hours

"Mom," I asked, "what do you want to do?"

She answered, "Let me get ready, and you can come pick me up. We will return to the hospital."

I called Jack back and told him what Mom had decided. "We are going to get Mom. We will meet you there as soon as you can get there." We let our girls sleep, and Brenda and I dressed quickly. As we stepped out of the motel, we discovered it was snowing. The streets were already covered with a blanket of snow. It was a beautiful but eerie night. We drove to the condo to get Mom. We arrived at about 1:15. She came out to the car, and we drove as quickly as we could back to the hospital. The roads were basically empty, and ours was a quick and easy drive. We arrived about 1:45 in the morning and checked at the front desk. One of the security guards met us and took us up to the fifth floor to Dad's room.

When we arrived at the waiting room, the security guard there told us that the doctor wanted to know when we arrived. I went into the unit to let them know we had arrived. She came out to give us an update.

Apparently, sometime around midnight Dad suffered two more attacks. A code blue was called. We had seen this happen a number of times while we were waiting. A voice over the intercom would begin to call for a doctor to come to a particular room and would keep saying it until everybody who needed to come had arrived. Sometimes the call would continue for five or ten minutes. It seemed that people would come from everywhere and go to the appropriate room to try to do whatever was needed to be done for a person who was perhaps dying. Dr. Judith said, "We lost him several times, but we resuscitated him. Each time, he came back. We lost him probably ten or twelve times.

The Passing Over of Dr. Jack Hyles

Each time we shocked him, on the very first time he came back. The infection in his lungs is also bad." She also mentioned that his blood pressure was dangerously low because of the excess lactaid acid in his blood.

Though she offered us very little hope, she added, "There is a nurse in there who is assigned to do nothing but try to keep him alive. We are doing all we can. We are trying everything possible to save his life, and we are in constant contact with his doctors." As people all over America slept, Dr. Jack Hyles was fighting for his life.

Jack and Cindy had arrived. It was interesting to me that at this point we were in a very uncomfortable waiting room, and we were so exhausted. We knew we could do nothing but wait. We gathered in the waiting room and tried to rest our eyes. Jack and I went into Dad's room, and we began to talk to him. I was amazed at how good he looked. After a surgery like this, I thought he would look much worse, but I also realized that he did look like he was near death. The nurse assigned to him was very, very diligent at trying everything possible to keep my dad alive. Knowing we were church people, he said to us in passing, "You know, I do not get to go to church very often; but this past Sunday I got to go to my Catholic church. The priest spoke on being a fisher of men. I came to work tonight and learned that I would be working on the ultimate fisher of men." It was apparent to us that this male nurse knew who Dr. Jack Hyles was and wanted to do all he could to keep him alive.

As we talked to Dad, we begged him not to die. We told him that we needed him, and we told him that Mom needed him. Soon after we arrived, Brother Colsten came. Perhaps the only man who was really with our family in the midst of everything

His Final Hours

was Brother Colsten; that was his job. I doubt that any of us really understood how difficult and grueling this was for him; after all, he had been working with my dad for over 35 years and loved him dearly. He was fearful that he was going to lose his boss, his pastor and his friend.

Jack and I asked Brother Colsten if we could anoint Dad with oil and pray for him. He went out to his car and brought back the oil; each of us put oil on our finger and prayed for him even as the nurses around us were working on him. Oh, how we pleaded with God to keep Dad alive and to heal him.

At this point in time, Dad's blood pressure was fluctuating. At a high, it would be 70 over 40, but then it would sink down to 50 over 40 or 60 over 30. It was dangerously low. The problem was that the kidneys could not flush out the lactaid acid because they had begun to fail. The nurse continued putting liquid in him to flush his system. Dad gained something like eight to ten pounds during these last hours of his life. On top of all his other problems, he now had kidney failure as well. We wondered if there was hope at all that Dad could possibly make it.

Mom never asked Dad to live. She sat in the waiting room most of the time, trying to catch a little sleep. She did come in every once in awhile to see what was happening. Finally, Mom made an incredible trip to Dad's room that I will never forget. We were all standing around Dad's bed, and it was obvious that all was not well. In fact, there seemed to be no hope. Mom reached down to take Dad's hand, and she said, "Honey, I do not want you to go, but it is okay. You can go; you have my permission." My heart broke. I did not want Dad to go; I did not think it was time for him, but Mom had already made peace with

The Passing Over of Dr. Jack Hyles

God about taking him.

. Mom then left the room. Jack and I remained, and suddenly Dad's blood pressure began to plummet. The alarm sounded for a code blue. We were asked to leave the room; people were in the room from everywhere. This time we saw the code blue for our beloved. We stood in the waiting room and watched people running from all directions toward Dad's room. For about 30 minutes we stood and waited for some kind of information as to whether or not he was going to make it. We were losing hope. It was finally beginning to sink in that Dad was going to die.

Finally, a doctor came out, introduced himself to us, and said, "We have tried everything we know to try, but his heart has failed. We have tried to bring him back, but he is not responding. We are going to give it another fifteen minutes, but if he does not respond, then there will be no hope that he will survive." The doctor went back in, and in about 15 minutes he returned. "I am so sorry, but there is nothing we can do. He is not responding. He is alive, but he is basically alive because of all the medicines that have been pumped into his body."

We were stunned. "He's gone?" My mind screamed. As I am sure confusion reigned in the minds of everyone, I did not know what to say or do. It made no sense. Dad wasn't supposed to die. It wasn't time for him to go. My mind was confused, as I am sure everyone else's mind was. Thousands of people, tens of thousands of people had prayed. We just knew Dad was still too needed. Our world was rocked at that moment beyond our wildest imaginations.

We asked if we could see him. We went tearfully into his room and gathered around his bed. We wept as we looked at him and knew these were the final moments; we were going to lose

His Final Hours

him. We still did not believe it could be true. Mom stood right next to him, holding his hand. After we said goodbyes to him, Mom began to sing, "In the sweet by and by, we shall meet on that beautiful shore; In the sweet by and by, we shall meet on that beautiful shore." No one else sang; Mom was the only one who was able to do so.

The doctor came to tell us that a decision had to be made. She wanted to know if Dad had expressed any wishes concerning keeping him alive by artificial means. I asked her one question, "Is there any possible hope that my dad could live?"

Sadly she said, "I am sorry, but there is no hope. He is being kept alive by these machines and the medication."

We all agreed that Dad would not want to be kept alive by artificial means. We requested a few minutes longer while other family members made their way to the hospital. Slowly the other family members arrived: his sister Earlyne; Jack and Cindy's children, Jaclynn and Kenny; our daughters, Amy and Bethany; and Jon and Teresa. We all gathered around his bed in his room to say goodbye. It was about 9:40 and time for the nurse to disconnect the different machines to let him go. Suddenly, Dad's blood pressure began to plummet, and he was gone. When they unplugged the respirator, Dad inhaled one last breath and died. It was 9:43 A.M., February 6, 2001.

We remained at his bedside for a few minutes weeping and just wanting a little last contact with him before we had to leave. Yes, his body was there, but his soul had gone on to Heaven. Looking back, I cannot help but believe that he had waited for Mom to say, "It is okay; you have my permission."

Somehow I believe when he said, "I am ready," he quit fighting, and the final "code blue" came. He did not wait for the

The Passing Over of Dr. Jack Hyles

machines to be unplugged; he died on his own. We were asked to leave the room so the tubes could be removed and all of the various machines could be disconnected. We went into the waiting room, made a few phone calls, prepared a statement, and tried our best to make some of the plans that needed to be made.

In a few minutes, they came and got us; we returned to his room. All of us had one last opportunity to say goodbye again. Soon those who loved him as pastor, as boss, as friend, as leader, and as a hero would begin receiving the news that Jack Hyles was gone.

6

Stunned!

*"The steps of a good man are ordered by the LORD:
and he delighteth in his way."*
(Psalms 37:23)

 E SORROWFULLY LEFT DAD'S room to begin an experience that none of us had anticipated—life without Jack Hyles. Our minds were dazed, our hearts were broken, and our eyes were swollen from crying. We were weary and overwhelmed with grief. We went back into the waiting room and tried to gather our thoughts as to what we were going to do. Many decisions had to be made, but there was much confusion in our hearts as to where to begin.

We also knew people were waiting for the news of Dad's condition. We began to make decisions as to how we were going to spread the word. If at all possible, we wanted the people of First Baptist Church of Hammond to be the first to know. We made this decision with the hopes that we would honor the staff

The Passing Over of Dr. Jack Hyles

and people of First Baptist Church. Therefore, we decided to immediately call First Baptist Church so that the church staff could be gathered together to hear the news. What transpired in that meeting can only be imagined. The heartbreak, like ours, was incredible. After all, these people had given their lives to Jack Hyles and served him for so many years. These folks rubbed elbows with him in the day-by-day business. They served with him, planned Pastors' Schools, operated the business of the church, and had literally lived and died to serve with their leader, Dr. Hyles. I am sure their reaction was similar to ours when we said goodbye to him.

Decisions were also made as to how to let all the schools and the college know. We made phone calls as quickly as possible to have various pastors and school administrators to go to the schools so that announcements would be made. At the same time, the reaction at each school was a great emotional outburst and tremendous grief. Brother Eddie Lapina met with the Hammond Baptist Junior High and High School and announced the news. He described it as the hardest thing he has ever had to do. He said that there was wailing and literal crying out in grief. For at least half an hour nobody could say a word. This same type reaction is exactly what transpired throughout all the ministries of First Baptist Church.

We knew that it was important to make contact with those around the country to let them know. We had tried to be very up front and honest throughout the ordeal. We never once tried to hide anything. Whenever we did not give complete information, it was because we did not have that information. In truth, many people did not know the severity of Dad's condition because we ourselves did not know how ill he was. It was never meant to be

Stunned!

a secret, nor did we ever intend to hide it. We simply gave the information as we received it.

We made a statement for the Internet site that had become a popular way for people around the country to find out was happening. (See Appendix 2.)

As we sat in the waiting room, Mom was visibly weak. We knew that she needed to eat, so we left to go to the cafeteria. Nobody was hungry, but we all knew that we were going to need the strength to make it through this day. We ate one of the most difficult meals of our lives in the cafeteria of the university hospital while Dad's body still remained upstairs in the ICU room where he had died. After eating, we made plans to meet back at Mom's condominium. As a family, we needed to begin dealing with the decisions that had to be made. There is no way humanly possible to describe the difficulty that we faced. Only with God's divine help were we able to deal with it. After lunch, we all went to our cars and left the hospital.

Shortly after noon, we all arrived at Mom's condominium. Mom made coffee, and we placed chairs in a circle in the living room. When everyone was there, we settled in and began deciding what to do. As any family who has lost a loved one, we faced hard decisions. Ours were no harder than anyone else's, but the magnitude of these decisions was beyond what most people would ever have to face. We were not dealing with the grieving of a handful of friends and relatives. We were dealing with the grieving of a church filled with people and a country filled with followers. I led our family in prayer, asking God to give us His wisdom and help. We all wept throughout this time of planning.

When we first began to discuss the plans for the funeral, it

The Passing Over of Dr. Jack Hyles

was very evident that Mom was struggling with something in addition to Dad's death. When we left the hospital and got into the car, Mom said, "David, who is going to preach Dad's funeral? I want you and Jack to say something, but who is going to preach it?"

I said, "Mom, nobody has to preach Dad's funeral. We can do anything with this funeral we want to do to honor him. Maybe we should just have a few people share their thoughts."

Mom's reply was, "I just do not want it to be a circus. I want it to be sweet. I do not want it to be some long drawn-out affair." Mom had seen funerals of other great men, and I knew she was bothered by some things done at these funerals. She did not want a bunch of big shots coming in and eulogizing her husband. She did not want Dad's funeral to be something where national fundamental leaders took charge, and we were left in their wake. She understood that these folks loved Dad, but this was personal. Mom's heart was really struggling with the thoughts that a conference atmosphere could begin at Dad's funeral.

As we planned the funeral, Mom's desires were to have it quickly and keep it simple. How do you keep the funeral for Dr. Jack Hyles simple? By this time basically the whole country knew of his Homegoing, and people were already calling and asking for information so that they could make travel arrangements. How in the world were we going to make plans to accommodate so many who needed to grieve, and yet keep it simple as Mom desired? Mom wanted the funeral on Thursday night and to be done with it. She said, "I do not want anyone coming to just gawk at Dad. I want it to be family." I could understand how Mom felt. Perhaps more than any of us, Mom needed time alone to grieve with Dad and for Dad.

Stunned!

God was so gracious to us. For as we talked, we began to come up with an idea that would do what Mom wanted, yet would satisfy all those who needed to grieve. We realized that there were three groups of people that needed to grieve. First and foremost, the family; secondly, and very importantly, the church; but thirdly, and not to be lost in all this, were people all across the country who still called him their pastor and preacher. How would we allow all of these folks to be a part and still keep it simple?

Finally, we arrived with the idea that we would have a Thursday night service for those around the country, and this would be a memorial service. It would be followed by a service on Friday morning for the church. Then the family would go to the cemetery for a time alone. This plan seemed to satisfy Mom; she could accept this. One of the moments of which I was most proud was when Mom said, "I want to speak on Thursday night and say a few words about Dad." It was evident that Mom had realized that the people who were coming really loved him.

Several decisions were made that were very important to us. One decision was that we wanted to have flowers sent. Dad loved flowers. Mom did not want some cold memorial; "We can take an others offering anytime," was her attitude. Another decision was to have a viewing that lasted for 24 hours, only to be interrupted by the evening memorial service. We also decided that Dad's viewing would be in the auditorium of First Baptist Church, the place that he loved so deeply. These were just some of the important decisions we made that day regarding the funeral arrangements.

We spoke about who would help in the funeral. Our desire was to involve the men who worked with Dad the closest at the

The Passing Over of Dr. Jack Hyles

church and the schools; involving men who so deeply deserved to be involved. We chose various men to speak, pray, read Scripture and to eulogize, as well as men to be the pallbearers. Finally, it seemed as though our plan was complete. Everyone was pleased; we knew God had given wisdom. We felt as though we had a plan that would work.

The first call we made was to Eddie Lapina, the Youth Director at First Baptist Church. We asked if he would come to the house to discuss these plans. After making further calls, it became evident that Thursday night was going to be too quick. There was a problem with properly preparing the body. We struggled with exactly what we should do. I said, "Mom, I know this is not what you want, and I know this is going to be tough for you; but there are a lot of things that cannot be ready by Thursday night. Can we please move it to Friday night and Saturday morning?" Mom very readily agreed for she had been pleased with the plans that had been made.

That evening Brother Lapina came to the house, and we discussed with him the plans. He immediately began to go to work to make things happen. I cannot fail to say that there was perhaps not a single man or person who did more to make the wishes of a family come true than Eddie Lapina, who only six months earlier had lost his own father. Though he was very tired, he worked to fill every wish that we had, and he, along with so many others, made everything that we desired come true to perfect fruition. Though he too was grieving, he lost himself in helping us.

After meeting with Brother Eddie, we got a call from Brother John Ault, the funeral director. I feared the thought of taking Mom to the funeral home. I had been there two years before

Stunned!

when our son passed away. I knew how grueling it would be for her. Brother Ault called and said, "Can I come to the house and meet with the family there?" How gracious! I knew that it would be much easier for Mom, so that evening Brother Ault and Brother Kimmel, his assistant, were to meet with us at 7:00 so that we could make the arrangements.

We all seemed comfortable with the decisions that were made. Mom ordered pizza; we didn't feel like going out and eating anywhere. We gathered around the kitchen and ate and talked and even laughed a little as we waited for the funeral director.

When Brother Ault arrived, we spent time together making plans and helping Mom make decisions concerning the casket and the flowers. Brother Ault and Brother Kimmel were a marvelous help in seeing that everything was as comfortable as possible. Truly we could see in advance that Dad was going to have a magnificent funeral, but, as Mom desired, it was not going to be circus. We were going to keep it simple—just simple in a grand way.

Many other things took place in the ensuing days. The next afternoon, we met together with all the men who would be involved in the funeral services. Each of them helped in arranging various parts of the services. The pallbearers were contacted, and all the details were being finalized. I cannot begin to express how much peace the family had knowing that so many people were working so hard to help honor our beloved. Although magnificent plans were made and tens of thousands of dollars were spent, the one wish that Mom had came true. She said, "I just want to keep it simple."

7

The Funeral Home

"A man that hath friends must shew himself friendly:
and there is a friend that sticketh closer than a brother."
(Proverbs 18:24)

OHN AULT, THE DIRECTOR of the Bocken Funeral Home, was a wonderful, dear friend throughout the difficult times of preparing for the funeral. It was overwhelming to ask all that we did of him. Yet, there was never a moment that he was not at the ready along with his wife and their assistant, Thom Kimmel, to do whatever the family asked or needed.

At the very beginning, Brother Ault was overwhelmed with the grief of losing his longtime pastor and friend. They had worked together many times in the past for other funerals. It is difficult to understand how a man could do as well as he did to understand the circumstances in which he found himself, but he was so professional and yet very personal in all that he did for us.

The Funeral Home

On Thursday evening, at 6:00, the family was to meet at the Bocken Funeral Home for our first viewing of Dad. The family members met at the Cracker Barrel on Kennedy Avenue and had dinner together before going to the viewing. It was a great time for family to be together, but we knew that it was going to be a very emotional time when we saw him for the first time.

In times of grieving, it is interesting the things that bring a sense of relief and comfort to you. I have learned so much about grieving in the past two years. I have learned that a person needs times of reflection to ponder his relationship with the one who is gone. That is exactly what happened to me both at my son's viewing and my dad's viewing. I am grateful that we had an opportunity to view Dad privately as a family. I believe it helped all of us to prepare ourselves for the services that were to come.

Brother Ault did a marvelous job in preparing the body of my father. He cared for every meticulous detail. Mom had chosen the suit and the tie that she wanted Dad to wear. She forgot a handkerchief, but Brother Ault knew that Dad often wore a hanky in his suit pocket, so he asked for a hanky to be sure that we had Dad dressed exactly like he would have dressed himself. He was able to put Dad's rings on his hands even though Dad had gained 20 pounds of fluid in the last days. We were very pleased with how he had prepared Dad's body for the viewing. It was far above our expectations.

When Dad first died, Brother Ault felt that there was a possibility that we might not want to have an open casket and that we would not even want to view him ourselves. Dad had gained a lot of weight because of water retention, and Brother Ault was afraid that we would be disappointed. We were sure that we wanted a viewing no matter what. It was, of course, our

The Passing Over of Dr. Jack Hyles

hope and our prayer that Dad would look as much like himself as possible, because Mom really understood how important it was for people to come by and see him one last time. I cannot explain why, but Mom knew that people needed that opportunity. She knew that people needed to see Dad's body and to make peace that he was gone. She had already decided that no matter what, she wanted Dad to have a proper viewing.

We weren't sure of what to expect when we went in the room the first time. Mom decided to go in first. She spent a few minutes alone, and then the rest of us followed. Though it was difficult to see him, we were delighted and pleased to know that the body looked so much like Dad. As a family, we spent probably an hour or so at the funeral home. We would spend some time by the casket and reflect and then step away and sit and talk with one another. There was some laughter as we told stories about Dad, and there were many, many tears. It was a bittersweet time; a time that we, as a family, valued greatly and will always value. Though we did not find ourselves in a position we wished to be in, we certainly were grateful for the great job done by those who helped prepare Dad's body for the viewing.

CHAPTER

8

A Church and a Nation Mourn

"Blessed are they that mourn:
for they shall be comforted."
(Matthew 5:4)

ARRIVED AT FIRST BAPTIST Church at about 8:50 on Friday morning, February 9, 2001. I saw the hearse was already parked in front of the auditorium. The casket containing Dad's body had not yet been brought into the church auditorium.

I immediately came through the office area and the education buildings into the auditorium. I was overwhelmed by what I saw. Flowers were already everywhere; on the platform, in the choir loft, and even the side walls were already completely filled with floral arrangements. It was a beautiful sight! We had already met and determined that we would have some of the lights left off in the auditorium; and taped, orchestrated Gospel songs would be playing while people were viewing the body.

The Passing Over of Dr. Jack Hyles

When we planned the funeral, we felt that many people would love to come to the viewing; so we wanted to accommodate everyone possible. We determined that a 24-hour viewing would be the best way to handle this. Brother John Ault suggested that an honor guard could be formed to stand for 40 minutes at the casket during the viewing time. These men were chosen from the deacon board and the male employees of the ministries of First Baptist Church. The response to this idea was overwhelming; the men were thrilled to have a part in honoring their pastor. Two men stood at parade address on the left of the casket, and two men stood on the right side.

The men had to be available from 9:00 A.M. Friday until 10:00 A.M. Saturday. One man stayed the entire 24-hour period in case someone was hindered from taking his place, but he was never called upon—what loyalty. The four men met in the main aisle 15 minutes before their shift was to begin, walked forward, two abreast, to dismiss the previous honor guards. The honor guards were asked to smile and acknowledge people but to carry on no conversations. Two security guards also stood by Dad's casket throughout the same 24-hour period. Their shift changes came at different times from the honor guards.

The pallbearers were at the front of the auditorium, awaiting instructions. We had chosen these men from various ministries. They were: Jesse Browning, Craig Bush, Randy Ericson, Victor Hernandez, Bob Hooker, and Bill Schutt. We also wanted to be sure that we had a group of honorary pallbearers who would include leaders of various ministries of First Baptist Church of Hammond. Our honorary pallbearers were: Bob Auclair, Don Boyd, Dave Douglass, Darrell Moore, Mike Sisson, and Tom Vogel. In addition, we had decided that the men who had been

A Church and a Nation Mourn

at the hospital on security would be the pallbearers with the family when we took Dad's body to the cemetery. These men were: Rick Bartley, Dale Breed, Lee Comstock, Mark Crockett, Phil Edge, Dave Sisson, Scott Tremaine, Clyde Wolfe, and Cliff Wroe.

Brother Jack Schaap arrived shortly thereafter, and we were asked to come to the back in order to accompany Dad's casket. Jack and I slowly led the way down one of the angle aisles, and behind us the men rolled the casket containing the body of my father. We walked to the front of the auditorium where the casket was positioned. Stage ropes were placed around the casket so that people could not get too close to Dad's body. As we were setting up, flowers were continually brought in—sometimes 10 or 15 arrangements at a time.

After we reached the front, Brother John Ault and his assistants prepared Dad's body and arranged everything to be exactly as we would have liked it to be. We placed a large 20 x 24 picture of Dad and Mom on his chair so that as people came in, they would see his picture in that place where he had sat so many times as pastor of First Baptist Church of Hammond.

About 9:15 that morning, the church staff members were given the opportunity of a semi-private viewing. These people had worked so closely with Dad over the years. Mom had mentioned that she would like to come and be there when the staff arrived. I called her a little earlier, and she was not sure she wanted to come; but when I told her how beautiful it was with the flowers and so on, Mom felt compelled to come to the church and see. She arrived shortly after the church staff had finished viewing.

Jack and I stood by the body as each church staff member

The Passing Over of Dr. Jack Hyles

came by. Their hearts were obviously overwhelmed with grief as each one now saw Dad for the first time since he had left the office on Friday. It had to be a very shocking moment. Practically every staff member said, "He went away, and he just did not come back." The whole scenario was a shock and a difficult experience for them; they never expected to lose their pastor, their boss, their fellow laborer. Most of them were sobbing as they went by.

Many of the staff members just stayed around in the auditorium for quite a while. When my mom arrived, I escorted her up the aisle. She began to weep even before we arrived at the casket. I think the finality was beginning to sink in for all of us. For several minutes we stood together at the casket and viewed Dad's body together. It is amazing how precious those moments and how timeless those moments remain—just having the opportunity to be near him. Mom went behind the ropes and patted his hand and kissed him. This was a sweet moment in a very, very grieving time. I was pleased because Mom was so happy with the way everything had been arranged. The flowers were a great comfort and thrill to her heart. She stayed for a few minutes, and then she left before the main viewing began.

The crowd had already begun lining up on the sidewalk to begin the viewing that was to start at 10:00. The honor guard was in place as well as the security personnel. The weather looked like it was going to become a treacherous day. The forecast called for rain that would soon turn to ice and snow. Definitely, we were facing a very dreary day. At 10:00 the doors opened, and the crowd began to come.

An amazing array of people came through to view Dad's body that day. Dr. Russell Anderson, Dad's dear friend and

A Church and a Nation Mourn

cofounder of Hyles-Anderson College; Brother Jack DeCoster, another great supporter and lover of Dr. Hyles; Dr. Tom Malone, Dr. Joe Boyd, Dr. Lee Roberson, hundreds and hundreds of preachers, laymen from churches all across America, missionaries from around the world, and members of First Baptist Church by the hundreds walked by the casket during the 24 hours Dad's body was lying in state. Also amazing was the number of people who came to view the body from the local area—literally hundreds of business people, neighbors from Mom and Dad's condominium, and nurses including one of his newest friends, John. All day long a steady line of people waited to view his body; thousands came to pay their final respects. People who were not even saved were compelled to be there because they wanted to be a part of this event and share their respect for this great man—my father.

In spite of inclement weather, we were all privileged to be part of a truly amazing day. Many people stayed all day long; some found their seats for the evening memorial service and remained there the entire day so that they would have a close seat and be a part of this never-to-be-forgotten occasion.

I am sure many stories could be told about Dad's viewing. I believe the most important thing to say is that it was a great honor to a man who so much deserved to be honored.

9

The Memorial Service

*"They shall abundantly utter the memory
of thy great goodness."*
(Psalms 145:7a)

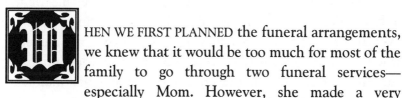 HEN WE FIRST PLANNED the funeral arrangements, we knew that it would be too much for most of the family to go through two funeral services— especially Mom. However, she made a very interesting decision; she decided that she wanted to say a few words at both services; however, she wanted only to attend one service. That evening, February 9, 2001, at 7:00, we had Dad's memorial service.

I must, at this point, express a word of gratitude to so many people who literally worked around the clock to prepare for the viewing as well as both services. Brother Eddie Lapina and his workers, as well as many others, did incredible things to make sure that we had everything the way we wanted it. The people of

The Memorial Service

the church and the staff pulled together in an amazing way to honor Dad, but to also honor the wishes of Mom and family. We planned for the Friday evening service to be somewhat more directed toward people from all over the country. We were thrilled at the crowd of people. Not only was the auditorium jam-packed with extra chairs everywhere, but people also packed the hallways, the mezzanine, and the closed circuit area behind the mezzanine and above the hallways, as well as completely filled the chapel and fellowship hall where the service could also be viewed on close circuit television. Many people who had come left because there was no room for them. It seemed that people came from every state and many foreign countries for the service. I noticed some very interesting things about the crowd.

Forgive me for these next few thoughts, but I believe they are very appropriate to this book. Sitting in the service that night were men that my father loved—men who had worked and served with him in days gone by. These men had been his friends in his earlier ministry but had slipped away from him a little bit over the years. There were men who had changed some and men who were associating with crowds whom my dad would not have chosen for them. Yet, there were two common denominators— these men loved my dad, and my dad loved them. Men sat in the First Baptist Church auditorium who hated each other; some men were present who would have destroyed another one present. Men attended who had voted each other off of boards and who had written articles about each other. That incredibly diverse group had one thing in common—they were mourning the loss of Dr. Jack Hyles.

I will not begin to share all of my thoughts, but I will just simply say that it is amazing that finally men that my dad loved

The Passing Over of Dr. Jack Hyles

but hated each other were together in one room, and it was accomplished by his death. Our desire in planning the funeral was that Dad be honored. Yes, I will admit that people were in attendance that we, as a family, felt had not been loyal to Dad, but he loved them. We made conscious decisions to be gracious and kind to every person.

We made decisions also as a family that even if we felt the person was not a friend, we would not do anything to hurt him; but we wanted to protect that person. We knew that any hurtful strife would be a dishonor to the way Dad had lived his life, for he always loved his enemies.

Also in planning this service, we wanted to make sure that it had a little bit more of a flavor of Dad's national ministry. Most of the people who came were from around the country, but many were Hyles-Anderson students. For that reason, we chose Dr. Wendell Evans to be the moderator and the song leader for this service. We felt that Dr. Evans having national exposure would be perfect for this, and we were right. As speakers, we chose men who also had a national exposure: Dr. Jeff Owens, Dr. Ray Young, as well as Jack Schaap and myself.

One of the first things that Mom knew she did not want was a camp meeting atmosphere with preaching, and she did not want a rah-rah spirit. She knew people needed to grieve; she understood that desire. She did not want the memorial service to just be a shouting service about Heaven. She wanted people to be able to express their sorrow and pain together for the loss of someone they loved so dearly. It was not a gruesome, morbid type of service, just a time when we were honoring someone we all loved and for whom we felt a great loss.

The music and every part of the service were just as Mom

The Memorial Service

desired. However, I feel the highlight of the whole service was after I introduced my mother, and she came from the choir waiting room and walked onto the platform before that crowd.

Yes, it was a funeral, but all of those present who desperately needed to express their love to her, rose to their feet and applauded her, as she so much deserved. I am amazed at my mother. To say that I was proud of her that night would be an understatement of the greatest magnitude, and I want to share with you the text of exactly what my mother said to that great crowd in that memorial service.

I asked to speak a few words to say thank you for coming. Many of you came from great distances and at great expense. Thank you for the flowers which are so beautiful. Brother Hyles loved flowers. We especially enjoyed flowers and trees on our recent trip to Hawaii.

Someone has said, "To the world you may be just one person, but to one person, you may be the world." My husband was my world. It was God's plan that I share my world with the world. Would we do it again? Yes! He loved the world and serving people. When he had to say "no" to someone, it hurt him.

All the newspapers and reports of all kinds said he died of complications of a heart attack. I believe he died of a very tired, weary heart. He had given and given. He loved giving. One of our nieces saw him sign Bibles for two hours after preaching a hard sermon. Use what you learned from him wisely for it truly came from God. He knew God. He walked with his God. Don't waste his life. Thank you. —Beverly Hyles

The Passing Over of Dr. Jack Hyles

The rest of the service was exactly what we wanted it to be, with the playing of "Amazing Grace" by a bagpiper in full regalia to end the memorial service. My dad had always loved hearing a bagpiper at the Hyles-Anderson College graduation because the college students are called "Hylanders."

I remember walking down the middle aisle for that memorial service with Cindy and her family and my family as well as many from my aunt's family that attended that memorial service. I remember sitting there, looking at, seeing the open casket, and wondering how I could make it through the service. At first it was very, very difficult, but God gave a tremendous amount of strength to all of us who were present that first night.

The service lasted about two hours, and without a doubt, what we wished to be accomplished was accomplished in that service. Again, I cannot begin to say how grateful we, as a family, were for all the efforts and all that was done to make that service truly an honor to our dad.

Just a portion of the flowers lining the walls

10

The Day of the Funeral

"But I would not have you to be ignorant, brethren,
concerning them which are asleep, that ye sorrow not,
even as others which have no hope."
(I Thessalonians 4:13)

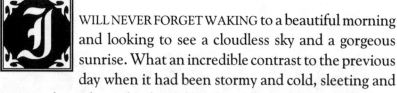 WILL NEVER FORGET WAKING to a beautiful morning and looking to see a cloudless sky and a gorgeous sunrise. What an incredible contrast to the previous day when it had been stormy and cold, sleeting and raining throughout the day. Though it was a cold morning, I was so grateful to God for giving us this beautiful day to lay Dad's body to rest.

The family was scheduled to meet at Mom and Dad's condominium at 9:00 that morning. We would be together as an entire family for the first time through this entire ordeal. This opportunity would be the first for everyone to be in town and at the same place at the same time. It was an amazing time when

The Passing Over of Dr. Jack Hyles

we were all finally together.

At about 9:15, we all went downstairs and got into the vehicles and were driven to the church. Eight limousines from the local car dealership were provided to us free of charge. Tyson Lincoln Mercury who did all the work for the leased vehicles for the church so graciously allowed these to be used. The drivers of these limousines had been the guards at the hospital and would also serve as the pallbearers at the cemetery. When we arrived, we went upstairs to room 200 in the Educational Building where we would wait until it was time to be taken into the auditorium for the funeral service. While we were there, a photographer from the church set up to take pictures of the family. How happy we were to have pictures taken together for the first time in many, many years.

About five minutes before the funeral was to begin, Mr. Ault came to get the family. We walked down the stairs and to the middle aisle in the back of the auditorium. I took Mom's arm and walked her as Mr. Ault led our family down that middle aisle. The casket now was closed for this service. We walked to the front and filled the first four rows with our family members. The crowd once again was jam-packed, but this was a different crowd; this was the home crowd. The First Baptist Church people had gathered to say goodbye to their beloved pastor.

Having spoken in both services, I can attest to the difference in the atmosphere. I felt a distinct difference in the way people were grieving. These folks were his people; he had fed them and pastored them. He had been there when their babies were born, he had counseled them, he had married them, he had buried their loved ones, and he had stood behind the pulpit and tried to touch their lives. This was a very grieving group of people that

The Day of the Funeral

day. Their preacher was gone and was not going to come back. It was a very difficult service; it was much different than the previous night.

We chose Brother Eddie Lapina, who had grown up at First Baptist Church, to be the moderator for this service. We would not have as many speakers for this service, but once again Mom decided to stand and speak to this crowd. Once again, she touched the hearts of the people there; I believe it was the highlight of the service.

I believe the greatest Christians in the world are the members of First Baptist Church. Brother Hyles loved being a pastor. That was one of his favorite words. On this corner, a group of the greatest people in the world serve. I've lost my best friend, my sweetheart, but we have all lost our pastor. He was my pastor of 54 years. He fed me; he sometimes scolded me through his sermons. But whether it was loving or exhorting, we knew he loved us.

God told me that Preacher would go to Heaven on February 6. I had been saying over and over, "The steps of a good man are ordered by the LORD," and I knew he had taken his last steps. I didn't want him to go, but God knows best. He called me in on Sunday and told me where my birthday presents were. He had prepared for my Valentine's Day.

This church will go on. Some say it was built on a man, but it was built on the Truth that man preached. It's stood over 100 years, and it will go on.

I've watched our young men and older men alike who

The Passing Over of Dr. Jack Hyles

*followed Brother Hyles so faithfully. We are in good
hands for the future. Thank you for holding us up in
your prayers. A special thanks also to John Ault who
always does such a good job.*

—Beverly Hyles

Dr. Evans also spoke for this service. Keith McKinney was
asked to read a eulogy and pray; he could barely speak as he
stood there and sobbed trying to eulogize his pastor. My dad was
the only pastor Brother McKinney had ever known since he was
five years old.

The music was sweet. One of Dad's favorite singers, Bill
Burr, sang. Barbara Burke, a soloist and member of First Baptist,
sang the song, "Here He Comes," accompanied by an adult
ensemble from the church. She also sang a song written by my
sister Becky called "The Sun Will Shine Again." That song
seemed to be a very appropriate choice for it was also sung at the
funeral of our son, Jack David.

When the service was over, the bagpiper once again walked
slowly to the front and played "Amazing Grace." As he played,
Mr. John Ault came and took the flag from the casket, and while
weeping himself, he handed the flag to my mother. As the casket
was prepared to be taken out of the auditorium, we waited,
watched, and listened to "Amazing Grace" being played.

The funeral was sweet; we had pleased Mom once again. She
was satisfied with all that was said and all that was done. The
most emotional moment I believe for all of us was to be the next
one. Mr. Ault came over to the family after the casket had been
removed from its pedestal and placed on the cart to wheel it out
of the church, and he asked the family to stand. I remember how

The Day of the Funeral

I felt as I followed Dad's casket out of the auditorium. We were all weeping. I realized this would be the last time that Dad would ever leave the First Baptist Church auditorium. Our hearts were breaking as we walked outside of the church building and stood as the pallbearers placed the casket into the hearse.

Many of the family members had left coats and belongings in room 200, so they began to go upstairs to get their things. The eight limousines were lined up behind the hearse, but several minutes passed before we were ready to leave. People began to spill out of the auditorium and began to gather along the sidewalks. Hundreds and hundreds of people who had been in the service waited for a glimpse of their preacher being driven away for the last time. I remember looking at the faces of the stricken people and wondering what they must be feeling. I could see so much sorrow and fear in their eyes; and even though I was grieving, I knew how their hearts must be breaking.

Finally, after several minutes we were ready to go. Quietly and almost reverently, hundreds of people packed the sidewalks, stood quietly, and watched the funeral procession leave. Most wept, some saluted, some waved, but each person in his own way said goodbye to his preacher as we left for the cemetery.

The trip to the cemetery was memorable because the Hammond police lined up to escort us the entire way. Eight police squad cars, numerous motorcycles, and auxiliary police cars escorted us, not just to the outskirts of Hammond, but all the way into Memory Lane. They stayed with us for the entire 35-minute drive, blocking every intersection. I believe this escort was their way of honoring a man who had truly influenced their city, and I remember thinking as we were driving, "Dad would be pleased, and he certainly earned this great honor."

The Passing Over of Dr. Jack Hyles

God was good to us, but how could a funeral service be perfect when the very nature of it is imperfect? I must say that we were pleased when that which we feared so much—not wanting to make it a spectacle or a three-ring circus, and yet wanting to honor all those who loved him—had turned out so perfectly. We were so thankful to the Lord for giving us the wisdom to do what seemed to be best to honor a man who deserved to be honored.

*Just a portion of the flowers which filled the
Educational Building lobby*

11

A Family Says Goodbye

*"And God shall wipe away all tears from their eyes;
and there shall be no more death, neither sorrow,
nor crying, neither shall there be any more pain:
for the former things are passed away."*
(Revelation 21:4)

HEN WE FIRST MET at Mom's condominium just a couple of hours after Dad went to Heaven, we faced some very difficult decisions. Probably the most difficult decision was how to give everyone the chance he needed and deserved to say goodbye to Jack Hyles. I am sure our inclination for selfishness was understandable. We had given him away all those years and had shared him with so many, and we desperately did not want to share him when it was time to say goodbye. Our better judgment won, and we made decisions to accommodate everybody; but we still knew there must be a time when we the family had him to ourselves.

The Passing Over of Dr. Jack Hyles

There were actually two such times; one was the first viewing on Thursday night, and the last would be the time in the cemetery. For obvious reasons, I will not divulge a lot of the details of that private time. Forgive me, but I have intimately shared the last days of my dad's life. However, I feel that most of the moments we had with him at the cemetery are too personal and precious to reveal in this book. Allow me to share a few thoughts regarding that time.

As I had mentioned previously, it was a beautiful day. We arrived in the beautiful sunshine at the Memory Lane Cemetery. The chairs had been arranged in a semi-circle. Jack and I had gone out ahead of time and decided to prepare the room that way. Since there was no speaker, a podium or even a place for a speaker to stand was not needed at this service. The casket would be at the head of that semi-circle near the place where Dad's body would be placed in a crypt.

Each car pulled up to the front door of the mausoleum, and each driver allowed us to get out and go inside until all of us finally were together. Obviously, some times of tears and sadness were mixed with laughter as we shared and remembered stories about Dad. Each of us was allowed to say goodbye in whatever way was best for us. We touched his hand, his face, looked at him, and wished we never had to say goodbye.

After about an hour, we knew it was time. We gathered all together around the casket and watched as Mr. Ault removed Dad's rings and glasses and handed them to Mom. Then we watched as they prepared him for the casket to be closed.

Brother Kimmel allowed me to be the one to seal the casket of my dad. I remember we wept as we stood there and took one last glimpse. When the casket was sealed, his sons-in-law and

A Family Says Goodbye

grandsons acting as pallbearers lifted his casket to the opening of his crypt and placed it inside. A curtain that had covered that spot was now gone. We stood there after the casket was inside and pondered for just a few moments all that had transpired the previous days. After a few minutes, we all left and walked back to the cars. We were driven to a restaurant to spend a time of fellowship as a family.

When the dinner was done, the family went to the condominium where all of the live floral arrangements had been brought. There were dozens and dozens of them. Each member of the family picked out one or two that they could take with them as a keepsake of the memorial and funeral services. We fellowshipped for a while until we all knew that we were so tired, and the time came to go. We left to go our separate ways. Mom was worn out, and she desperately needed rest.

Brenda, my two girls, and I left Mom to drive back to the Residence Inn where we had first checked in on the day we arrived, when Dad was at Broadway Methodist. To get there, we had to drive right by the cemetery. The cemetery had been closed for the entire day; no one was allowed to come or go. We were so grateful for the graciousness and kindness shown in protecting the privacy of the family.

Brenda, our girls, and I drove into the cemetery and pulled up at the mausoleum. No one was there of course except the security guards, and they were stationed outside. We unlocked the door and went inside. The letters had already been affixed to the marble stone. I remember walking in and seeing the sight. My heart was torn out as much as anything for there, side by side, were two of the most important men in my life. One was my father, Jack Hyles, and next to him my little boy, Jack David

The Passing Over of Dr. Jack Hyles

Hyles. I stood there and cried along with my wife and daughters as two very precious people in our lives had left us in less than two years. My heart was filled with grief at the thought of losing both of them.

*The crypts of my dad and our son
at Memory Lane Mausoleum*

His Last Words

*"A word fitly spoken is like apples of gold
in pictures of silver."*
(Proverbs 25:11)

 HEN I BEGAN TO work on this book, this chapter was not a part of my plan. I had decided that I would not have one chapter dedicated to the various final words of my dad's life, but something happened that made me feel that this chapter needed to be included.

After Dad's death, obviously I felt a great responsibility to make sure that my mom was well cared for and that she had the attention that she needed. Beyond doubt, no one could take Dad's place, but I knew that I needed to give my mom a lot of attention and love as well as help her in any way that I could. To do that, I began to call her at least once or twice every day, and sometimes more, just to check in with her and to be sure that she was all right. Being the only son, I felt a certain obligation, and

The Passing Over of Dr. Jack Hyles

this was an obligation I was delighted to fulfill.

A month and two days after Dad's death, I called Mom on the phone. She said, "David, I had an incredible thought last night. I could not get away from it." At first her words scared me. I thought maybe something was wrong with Mom or there was a problem—something she had left undone or some fear.

I asked, "Mom, what is it?"

"David, as far as we know, the final words Dad ever spoke were, 'I love you, John.' " When my mother told me this, I knew what she was thinking. She continued, "David, Dad died loving, and even when he was going into surgery, he felt the need to tell someone that he loved him."

May I share something interesting about this? The final "I love you" that Dad ever spoke on this earth was not to his wife of 54 years. It was not to his son or his daughters, though he told us that he loved us as well. It was not to his grandchildren or his sister, nor to the dedicated, loyal men who worked by his side for so many years, though he told all of these folks that he loved them. His final "I love you" was to a man he barely knew.

There may not be anything more significant about my dad's life than the simple fact that he loved deeply and he loved quickly. Mom put it this way, "Dad simply loved people, and he had to express that love before surgery."

Forgive me, but a part of me wishes that I had been the last person to whom Dad said, "I love you." A part of me feels jealous for Mom that she was not the last recipient of those precious words. I believe I understand how Mom felt when this eye-opening thought came to her because it makes me even more proud of my father.

A male nurse came into his life; that nurse served him, took

His Last Words

care of him, and met the needs that he had while he was in pain and suffering in the hospital. They struck up a friendship just like Dad did with everyone whether for just a few minutes in and out of an elevator or at a table having a dinner. As that friendship was struck, Dad saw a human being, a life, and a soul. In the course of that relationship, he looked inside the heart of a fellow human being and loved him.

This is what really struck my heart when the beloved disciple John was describing Jesus. John referred to himself as the disciple Jesus loved. His name was John, and he knew Jesus loved him. Obviously Jesus expressed His love to him. When Jack Hyles died, he expressed his love to a young man named John as well.

Something else interesting about this time was how Dad told John that he loved him. He reached up, grabbed the head of that nurse, and pulled him down to say, "John, I love you." He showed affection, a deep, heart-felt compassion for that nurse. He touched that nurse's life because he chose to love him. He did not look at that nurse as someone who would simply tend to him in a room; he looked at that nurse as he looked at every human being he had ever met—someone who needed to be loved.

Jack Hyles loved people. Who did he love? He loved the rescue mission men and formed some dear friendships with men who had fallen on hard times and had stumbled into the rescue mission he founded. He loved the poor ghetto child. He saw himself in them. No child ever came to First Baptist Church from the ghettos who was not loved by Jack Hyles.

He loved the broken; no life was too broken to receive his love. No one had fallen too far but what he would love him or her. He loved the teenager. Even at 73 years of age, he stood at

The Passing Over of Dr. Jack Hyles

Youth Conference and poured out his heart because he loved teenagers. He loved the college students who came from all over America. Some were brash, obnoxious, and sometimes irritating, but never to the extent of their not being loved by my dad.

He loved the senior saints. There was always warmth for them in his heart from the time he was a very young pastor until he himself was a senior saint. How he loved those who were elderly. He loved the blue-collar man, the steel-mill worker, the factory worker, the construction worker, the janitor, and every other man who labored in circumstances that perhaps he might not have preferred. Dad loved the men and felt their hearts. He loved families. He delighted in marrying their children, providing schools in which to rear them, and even being there in their times of grieving.

He loved the businessman—no matter who he was or how wealthy he was. Dad loved him not for his money or his wealth or his power or his fame, but because the rich man was also a human being who needed his love.

He loved his neighbor. Those who came in day-to-day contact with Jack Hyles felt his love. In fact, he had become a presence to all of those who were at the condominium where he lived, and they too felt a sense of loss and grief when they heard the news that he had died.

He loved the stranger. So many times I would be with Dad, and when his path crossed someone's in just everyday life, he could see that person's heart. A casual watcher could almost see Dad's love instantly emanate toward that human being.

He loved his people; Jack Hyles worked harder perhaps than any other preacher has ever worked preparing for the people at the First Baptist Church in Hammond. Oh how he loved them!

His Last Words

When he stood in his pulpit, his heart ached to meet their needs. He wished that he could have been closer to each member, but he loved them sincerely and deeply.

He loved preachers. Very few preachers in history had as great a burden and heart for other preachers as my dad had. So many times when he was tired and weary from carrying the load of his own church, he would bear the load of another preacher because he loved him.

Dad loved the churches. When Jack Hyles went to another church, he took his heart with him; and while he was there, he gave it to those to whom he was ministering. People would come to hear him preach who had never before heard him and would leave feeling loved. What a capacity he had to love the churches.

He loved his enemies. Volumes could be written about what Jack Hyles did for those who sought to hurt him. Volumes could be written of the kindness he showed to people who even tried to destroy him. Jack Hyles did not just love those who loved him; he loved those who hated him. Even his enemies could not escape his love.

He loved those who served with him. The staff, the faculty, and the administrators of his schools and college—all were deeply loved by their boss. I stood at the casket a little after 9:00 that Friday morning when the church staff walked by before the regular viewing began. I watched pastors, secretaries, and janitors walk by weeping as they looked into the casket at the body of a man who had loved them dearly, and they knew it. He loved them when they did not do a good job. He loved them not just because of all the good things they did; he loved them because they were human beings who worked with him.

On the last Friday before he went into the hospital, a very

The Passing Over of Dr. Jack Hyles

strange event took place. Dad had gone to the office that morning to work for a while. Something had taken place in the office with a staff member, and he had to severely scold that staff member. The staff member had let him down in a major way, and it hurt the work in some fashion. Dad scolded the staff member severely. When he came home, he told Mom about it. When we were recounting it she said, "David, it hurt Dad's heart. He was sad. He loved that staff member so much he hated having to scold him." This incident is just an example of how much he loved those who worked with him.

He loved his family. I would never be able to tell in this book all of the many ways Dad showed his love. I cannot tell of the love he showed to those of us who had the incredible honor of being a part of his family. Dad expressed his love by giving of his time—quality time. Sometimes he was so busy that he could not give us the time that he would have loved to give us at a particular time. However, because he gave us such quality time, it was less difficult for all of us because we felt so loved by dad, or husband, or brother, or grandfather. If any one of us had a need in our lives, Dad would meet it. His generosity permeated in a special way to those of us in his family.

And so, Jack Hyles died loving. I sometimes wonder if a human being existed on God's earth who could have escaped his love. I never knew a man or a woman whom my father hated. I do not think I could think of any he did not like. Yes, some disappointed him greatly and some he did not trust, but none existed whom he did not love. As I close this chapter, picture in your mind this beautiful scenario.

He has just said goodbye to his family. Doctors and nurses surround him as they walk him through the corridors of the

His Last Words

University of Chicago Hospitals. They are leading him to a place that holds great fear for him—the surgical room. In a few moments, the doctors are going to open his chest, go inside of his heart, and perform a very delicate operation. Anesthesiologists are going to put him to sleep, and he does not know if he will ever wake up. He has no clue as to his own future; his destiny is not in his own hands. For one of the few times in his life, he has no control; others have control.

He has been in his hospital bed for almost a week. He is in more severe pain than anyone knows. He is weary and struggling for breath; every negative emotion a person can feel, he is feeling. He has said goodbye to his wife of 54 years, not knowing if he will ever see her again on this earth. He said goodbye to children, grandchildren, and his only living sister. His assistant pastors have prayed with him, and he does not know if he will ever again see those men or those others who worked with him. He has walked out of the pulpit of First Baptist Church perhaps for the last time and does not know if he will ever return.

He does not know if he will wake up with his earthly family surrounding him or if he will wake up with his Heavenly family surrounding him. He does not know if he will wake up to talk *about* Jesus or wake up to talk *to* Jesus. He does not know if he will be coming back to recovery or entering into eternity. He is unsure, unsteady, and unable to know what lies ahead.

That which Dad has dreaded for so long has now finally found its way into his life. He never wanted to know that he had a heart problem. He never wanted to know that he had blockage. He never wanted to enter into this place called surgery. None of this upset was part of his plan.

Imagine his lying there just outside the door. In only a

The Passing Over of Dr. Jack Hyles

second, that door will open, and he will be in the hands of those who will do their best to save his life. In most cases, total strangers walk beside him. Walking beside him is John, a young nurse he has known for six days. John, a strong, athletic, fine-looking young man has done his best to take care of his patient. They laughed a little bit, perhaps cried a little bit, and no doubt, John was there for him in some very hard and difficult suffering moments. Now, he looks up to see his last familiar face on this earth—though familiar for only a few days.

Picture in your mind the self-pity he might have had. Picture the feeling sorry he could have done. Imagine all of the emotions running through his mind as he reaches up his hand (which no doubt caused more pain) and grabs the back of the head of the male nurse. He pulls him down to say, "I love you, John." I am not sure how that young man must have felt, but maybe that young man experienced the strongest, sweetest love he had ever known. I know it was the godliest love he had ever known.

The young man was almost speechless, but he answered, "I love you, too." Imagine as the young man steps away from the bed, and no doubt the man in the bed gave him that signature smile as he was rolled away. John looked at another one who stood beside him and said, "That is a scared man." But then he added, "That is a good man."

As you picture this scene in your mind, do not forget that for most of Dad's life, through adversity, sorrow and pain, he always put aside himself and reached up to all of us who came into contact with him. Not only did he manage to tell us, but he made us believe that he loved us.

13

Why Did He Have to Die?

"Precious in the sight of the LORD
is the death of his saints."
(Psalms 116:15)

THE WORDS TO THIS verse have mesmerized my mind since the day Dad died. I believe they have held my attention because I have been seeking answers with so many others to the questions, "Why did Jack Hyles die? What was God thinking?"

A church was stunned and left without a pastor. A nation was stunned and left without a voice. A college was stunned and left without a chancellor. A school system was stunned and left without a superintendent. Bus kids were stunned and left without their hero. Pastors were stunned and left without the pastor of pastors. A sister was stunned and left without her brother. Grandchildren were stunned and left without their grandfather. Nieces and nephews were stunned and left without

The Passing Over of Dr. Jack Hyles

their uncle. Four children were stunned and left without their father. A wife was stunned and left without her husband. Why?

The word *precious* does not mean *sweet.* It is not a gooey word nor a word that means *fine, good,* or *okay.* Rather, *precious* is a very sophisticated word which means *to make rare, to be prized, to be set aside as a valuable.* We oftentimes talk about the meticulous care which God takes to craft the birth in the life of a human being. We speak of the marvelous, meticulous nature by which God crafts a baby in the womb. We speak often of God's concern with how He made us, but how easy it is to forget that God crafts the death of his saints with the same great care. It is meticulous, it is perfect, and it is set aside as valuable. We can see the handiwork of God in death just as much as we see the handiwork of God in birth.

With that definition of *precious* in mind, I decided to study the death of Jack Hyles with a different view. I decided to look at his death and analyze it as a jeweler would analyze a precious stone. I decided to analyze it like an archeologist would analyze a rare find. I decided to study it as a meteorologist would study a rare storm. I decide to put under the microscope the death of Jack Hyles, the precious, rare jewel that God made it to be.

Perhaps the first aspect that I had to accept was that God treated my dad's death with the same individual care with which He treated his life or his birth. When God made Jack Hyles, his birth was unique. His birth was crafted to create the man God wanted him to be. In the same way, his death was crafted to complete the man that God wanted him to be. God's care for his death was meticulous, personal, and was between God and my dad.

God did not look down from Heaven and say, "What if, uh-

Why Did He Have to Die?

oh, or well, I'll be..." Let me repeat, there was nothing about Dad's death that God did not perfectly craft. No doctors decided his death. No machines could decide his death. Surgery played no role, and it was not his heart; but it was a meticulously, perfectly, planned act of God to complete the man.

It is interesting to note that we oftentimes judge a man by his work; however, God judges the man by the man because the man is the work. For 74 years, God worked on Jack Hyles because Jack Hyles let Him. God crafted him through every little characteristic of his person and then crafted him through every virtuous quality. Finally God crafted Jack Hyles to complete him in his death.

Another aspect I began to see in the death of my dad was that it was not the work that God was considering; it was the warrior. I struggled so desperately to understand this, and I know that most people did the same. To me, Dad's death was untimely. To my sisters, Dad's death was untimely. For our children, Grandpa's death was untimely. To Earlyne Stephens, her brother's death was untimely. To the assistant pastors and staff people at First Baptist Church, their boss's death was untimely. To the members of First Baptist Church, their pastor's death was untimely. To the students of Hyles-Anderson College, their chancellor's death was untimely. To the students of Hammond Baptist Schools, their superintendent's death was untimely. To fundamental Christians across America, the death of their hero and leader was untimely. Still Brother Jack Hyles' death was exactly what God wanted for the man. I suppose the closest person to not accepting his death, but perhaps understanding its timeliness, was my mom.

I spoke to my mom a few days after Dad died. Though I had

The Passing Over of Dr. Jack Hyles

returned to Florida, I called her every day to chat. I checked to see how she was feeling, if she was doing all right, or if I could help her in any way.

On a day when Mom was grieving terribly, we were talking about Dad's death. I could feel the pain and loneliness in her voice. She was struggling to sleep well. Mom made several statements to me that were very significant. She said, "David, Dad was very, very tired. He felt like there was no way he could let go of the ministry. He struggled with the thought of someone else trying to pastor that great church and lead that great ministry. I think this was the only way. God knew that this was the only way that he would have his rest."

Interesting, isn't it? I believe that what was so hard for me and everyone else to understand (and seemingly so untimely), Mom understood that it was simply perfect timing for him. God crafted that time so carefully, and God did what was best for the man, not for the ministry.

Another aspect of the preciousness of Dad's death was that it was not what was best. I struggled in the early couple of days after Dad's death because I heard so many try to say, "This is the beginning of the greatest days for our ministry." No, no, that is not true. Reality is this: The greatest days of the ministries of my dad are over.

You say, "You are declaring doom and gloom upon the ministries of First Baptist Church, Hyles-Anderson College, and all of the many ministries of your dad."

No, I simply said, "The greatest days of my dad's ministries are over." Wait a minute and consider this with me. That simply means this: God does not use ministries; God uses people. If we spend our time merely perpetuating the ministry, it will die.

Why Did He Have to Die?

Rather we should perpetuate the will of God for each of our lives. In other words, each of us must do our best in that which God has given us to do. Certain elements will fade; certain elements of the ministry will prosper not depending on Jack Hyles, but depending upon the person who commits himself to that ministry.

It was difficult for me to understand how people could think that Dad's death was best for everyone. Dad's death was best for no one but Dad. It was not best for Mom; it was not best for me. It was not best for everyone else. It simply made each one of us decide whether or not we were going to be committed to our task at hand. His death has given us a goal of trying to be as committed to staying in the perfect will of God for our lives as Jack Hyles was for the 74 years he lived.

This point is very important to me. I had to come to the realization that Dad did not make any mistakes regarding his health. A lot of second-guessing goes on when a person dies in a way that my dad did. Some may ask, "Why did he not have surgery two years ago?" Others ask, "Why did the doctors not detect the massive problem with his heart earlier?" Another may ask, "What if he would have just taken better care of himself?"

Two years before my dad's death when the doctors told him he had problems with his heart, we did not know it, but God was already crafting, perfecting, preparing, and planning the death of His saint. I have had to come to grips with the fact that if Dad had undergone surgery earlier, he might have died on the operating table and lost two very valuable years. Perhaps Dad would have been an invalid, and the productivity of these two wonderful years would have been impossible. I believe that God knew, and God put in the heart of Jack Hyles to know that the

The Passing Over of Dr. Jack Hyles

decisions he made concerning his health were the decisions that would perfect what God was doing in his life. Dad finished his work. I cannot see it as finished, but God does. I had to come to grips with the fact that God put in Dad's heart to do what he did.

Think with me for a moment. There were so many times in Dad's life when those of us who followed him and worked with him could not understand his decision making, but we came to learn that what we did not understand was being done by a principle. These were principles that we oftentimes could not see until much further down the road. I believe Dad died with principles. Principles helped him in making decisions. Principles helped him to know what he should do, and that is exactly what he did.

I choose to believe that God led His servant from the moment Dad found out about his illness at the Mayo Clinic until he breathed his last breath. I believe that God helped him to know what was best and what was right. Why would God lead a man for 72 years to do His best and perfect will and abandon him the last two years? Why would God give this man wisdom to do all that he did through seventy-two years and leave him the last two years? I do not believe that is God's way. I believe that God also led him in the final two years of his life. God perfected the man and allowed the man to finish the ministry.

I have chosen to accept Dad's death. I did not accept as one who says, "I am ready," nor am I ready now. I chose not to accept his death as one who eagerly anticipated it or who readily accepts it now. I accept his death as being a rare jewel in the coffers of God's divine plan—a death that was perfectly crafted to be exactly what God wanted it to be.

Why Did He Have to Die?

Doctors, you have no blame. Nurses, you made no mistakes. Surgeons, your skills were not flawed. Family and friends, your acceptance of his decisions concerning his health were not selfish. We were all merely actors in the final play of the life of Dr. Jack Hyles.

If you will, take flight with me for just a moment, and let us try to somehow rise and see from a viewpoint next to God. He looked down at a man who had lived a life committed to Him. He was a man who perhaps for one day had never been out of the perfect will of God for his life. Meticulously, do you see Him working? He is finishing the man. God is putting on the finishing touches! God did so many things to finish him. On February 5, 2001, God looked down to Beverly Hyles and He said, "Beverly, I am going to take your husband tomorrow morning. It is time. He is finished. He is completed. I am going to take him whether or not you allow me to, but I would love to have your permission." That night Beverly Hyles looked up to her God and said, "I give my husband to you."

God then looked down at His unconscious warrior and said, "I know you will not go without permission; you will fight." So God said to Beverly Hyles, "Now, you need to give him permission." On February 6, 2001, Beverly Hyles went to the side of her husband and said, "It is okay; you have my permission to go." And God, Who needed no permission, allowed two of His own to submit to His will. When all was said and done, God said, "Okay Jack, when you are ready, come." Jack Hyles defied the machines and said, "Goodbye."

Look at it; it is perfect. It was not perfect to me or for me, not perfect for you, but perfect, precious, rare, and valued to Jack Hyles.

14

I'm Sure He Noticed

"Consider the lilies of the field, how they grow."
(Matthew 6:28b)

T WAS VERY RARE for Jack Hyles to overlook a kindness shown to him by anyone. Gratitude permeated his life. At a restaurant, he gave a more than gracious tip. The waitresses always loved serving him for he was never unkind or obnoxious. He would always show the utmost in graciousness and gratitude. Jack Hyles noticed any gesture of kindness. He often reached into his pocket to get a 3x5 card; inevitably, if it was not an idea for a sermon or something that needed to be done at the church, it was a note to remind himself to send a note of gratitude.

Dad loved to be loved. When we were at the hospital with him in the final days, he would often ask if people were wondering about him. He always wanted to know who was there and who had come to see him. He loved to be loved is the only

I'm Sure He Noticed

way I know how to put it. Expressions of love to him meant so much, and he made it easy for people to show those expressions of love. Anyone could afford a Reeses' Peanut Butter Cup, and he always appreciated every little expression of love.

When we were planning the funeral service, I already knew the answer to the question I was going to ask Mom, but I asked her out of courtesy. "Mom," I asked, "What about flowers?" Many times when a person dies, the family members ask for people to send a donation to some charity. I already knew what Mom would say because I knew what Dad would love. She answered, "Son, let them send flowers. Dad would have liked that." So we decided not to discourage people from sending flowers. The response to Dad's death was overwhelming. Thousands of letters and multitudes of phone calls and telegrams arrived. One of the sweetest and the most overwhelming happenings was the abundance of the floral arrangements that were delivered to the church. The church looked like a garden.

I decided in this book that we would do what Dad would do; we would say thank you to all of those who sent flowers. The platform, the choir, the walls from the front to the back of the auditorium, the vestibules, and every possible little place had a floral arrangement. Sometimes those arrangement were three and four deep. For Dad, I say, "Thank you for thoughtfulness and your kindness." I am sure that he looked down from Heaven; and if he could have, he would have taken a 3x5 card and a pen and written you a note to simply say, "Thank you for your kindness to me." (See Appendix 3.)

15

He Never Lost His Humor

"A merry heart maketh a cheerful countenance."
(Proverbs 15:13a)

VERYONE WHO KNEW JACK Hyles knew of that sparkle in his eye and that mischievous grin he would show every time he was teasing with someone. One of the interesting aspects about Dad is that to the very, very last conscious moment, he never lost his sense of humor nor his wit. He had a lot of fun with people; he liked people. He said it in the hospital, "I love people." His wonderful sense of humor would always make people feel comfortable with him.

Growing up in the Hyles' home was a battle of the wits, and it all began with Dad. He always had a smart crack, a funny insult, or teasing jabs. Even as a teenager, when I would bring someone new home, I remember Dad's trying out the same old jokes on the new person. As a teenage boy, if I invited a

He Never Lost His Humor

girlfriend over to eat, the second she would start putting food onto her plate, he would say, "Don't take so much; leave some for the rest of us." He would literally scare the girl to death, and my sisters got the same treatment with their boyfriends. He would disarm some young date of one of my sisters by literally passing a roll if the date asked for one. Dad would grab a roll and throw it to him. Oftentimes Dad's humor relaxed an otherwise tense situation with a young man who was scared to death of our dad!

Dad teased with everyone. When a waitress would come to the table in a restaurant, he would cut up with her. No matter where he went, his sense of humor was always evident. People liked him because the humor was obviously not a sarcastic humor but a loving humor. He kept that same delightful way throughout his stay in the hospital.

I felt this book would be incomplete without sharing some of the funny moments in the hospital. I want to share comments and statements Dad said that were filled with humor. It should also be noted that he kept the sparkle in his eye until the end.

When Dad first went into the hospital and realized that he had had a heart attack, his sister Earlyne came to his bedside. Dad told Earlyne a little bit about what had happened to him. Of course, she was deeply burdened and heartbroken because she knew her brother was extremely ill. They loved each other so very, very much. While she was standing at his bedside, Dad said to her, "Earlyne, when you went into the hospital with your heart problems, I prayed for you, and God answered my prayer. You were able to have a successful angioplasty procedure. I even kept you from having surgery. So, are you going to pray for me now that I am in the hospital?" Then he added, "Well, knowing

The Passing Over of Dr. Jack Hyles

the way you get prayers answered, it is probably better that you didn't!" After my dad died, my aunt retold that story several times with a big smile. She enjoyed the teasing of her brother and the relaxation he brought when confronted by a very difficult situation.

Several times when we were in Dad's room, he told jokes. He would tell a funny story, especially when we would bring in someone like one of the grandchildren. He shared several blonde jokes. He told one joke about a fellow who used his hearing aides in a unique way. I will not relate that joke here, but suffice it to say, it was funny, and it was family.

Every nurse who came and worked with Dad was subjected to some of his humor. I remember one nurse who came in and said, "Mr. Hyles, I do not want to make things uncomfortable for you." Dad replied with a semi-serious grin, "Then why are you?" She looked at him, startled at first, and realized he was kidding. A friendship formed almost immediately between Dad and that nurse. He liked them, so they liked him back. He was playful. Through all the pain that Dad was in, he never complained even when he expressed his discomfort. He told when he was in pain, but he kept his remarks above the level of whining or complaining; he also kept the humor going even when he was struggling with pain.

John, the male nurse at the University of Chicago Hospitals, and Dad had a lot of fun together. He was a relaxed kind of a professional guy. He and Dad teased a lot. One day John was telling Dad about how he had become a Certified Public Accountant, but he went back to school to become a registered nurse. Dad said to John, "John, you have got to wonder about a guy who would trade an accounting book for a bed pan." That is

He Never Lost His Humor

the kind of humor Dad shared with John. They cut up a lot with each other when Dad was in the hospital.

Brother Colsten came to pray with Dad before he went into his surgery. As Brother Colsten stood at Dad's bedside and prayed as he could so eloquently do, he asked God to be with my dad during the surgery. In his prayer, he prayed something like this, "Dear God, give my preacher what he deserves." When Brother Colsten finished the prayer, Dad opened his eyes, looked at him, and said, "Johnny, what is the matter with you? Are you mad at me or something? Asking God to give me what I deserve?" Again, he was always finding humor in every situation.

On the way to his angiogram, we were all scared to death that we were going to lose Dad. To be quite frank, Dad was very frightened. He knew he was facing an emergency procedure, and he knew that this was not supposed to happen yet. It was obvious to all of us that this was a very touch-and-go moment. We were walking Dad to the room where they would perform the procedure. Everyone had said goodbye and sort of lagged behind, but Mom, Cindy, and I stayed with Dad. Mom kissed him and said goodbye. Cindy kissed him on the forehead and told him that she loved him. As I mentioned previously, I was overcome with emotions and reached down and kissed him on the forehead and said, "I love you, Dad."

He looked up at me with a glimmer in his eye and said one word, "Yuck." Dad and I hugged each other often. We loved each other very much, but in a very serious moment in time, he found just a simple word to make us all smile—"Yuck." Though he was a man filled with fear, he never lost that humor.

When the angiogram was finished and Dad was made aware of his condition, I knew how heavy his heart was. We were all

The Passing Over of Dr. Jack Hyles

very frightened as well. We were waiting for the word to airlift him to the other hospital when I found it was my turn to go into his room. Brenda and I went in together, and I said, "Hey, Dad! How are you doing?"

He looked up at me with a very sad, somewhat pitiful, look and he said, "Well, I have a damaged heart. I have at least three blocked arteries. I have heart failure. I had a heart attack, and I have a bad valve, but other than that my heart is in great shape." He grinned the patented Jack-Hyles grin, but this grin had a little more pain and fear in it than any grin I had seen before.

When Dad was getting ready to say goodbye to us before surgery, we were all getting ready to see him conscious for the very last time. The entire family went into the room and gathered around his bed for a very sweet, intimate moment. At the very end of that visit, his last words were; "I love you. You are all a great bunch of people. Now get out of here before I start to cry." That big grin spread across his face, and we all chuckled and laughed as we left; but our hearts were aching. Somehow Dad had managed to inject just a little humor—something to make us all smile—as we walked out of the room and said goodbye to him for the last time he would share a conscious moment with us.

I close this chapter by saying I noticed something about Mom and Dad. When we walked into the room, Dad always tried to pep up a little and interject a little more humor. When Mom was in the room, there was not a lot of teasing. Dad would look at Mom a lot and smile a beautiful smile. She would pat him on the hand and talk to him in a very loving way. He would stare at her, and sometimes all he would do was just smile. I believe that there was something extraordinarily special between the two

He Never Lost His Humor

of them that needed no humor; there was no need to relax the other. Fifty-four years had brought to them a comfort zone that none of us could know. The tenderness and sweetness that they had enjoyed for numerous moments now communicated best by just a loving smile.

16

Jack David

*"...he shall gather the lambs with his arm,
and carry them in his bosom."*
(Isaiah 40:11b)

N THE FINAL HOUR of Dad's life, we stood around his bed knowing that very, very soon we would say goodbye to him. The sorrow and grief in our hearts was beyond words. I could not even imagine life without my dad. I am sure all the other family members felt the same. All night long, doctors labored to try to keep Dad alive. He was hooked up to an amazing array of medical marvels all being used to try to sustain his life; but they failed, and now they were merely holding him back temporarily.

The family members were on their way. The nurse came in and asked if we wanted to keep him alive or if we wanted to disconnect all the tubes and IV's to let him die. Of course, I asked the question, "Is there any hope?"

Jack David

Mom said, "Dad would not want to be kept alive if there was no hope." We requested that they not do anything until the rest of the family arrived. We stood around the bed until various members of the family came to be with us.

As we were standing by his bedside, only one thought of comfort came to my mind. Somewhere up in Heaven, a little five-year-old boy, or maybe seven now, who loved his grandpa very much waited for him.

On March 24, 1999, at the Mayo Clinic in Rochester, Minnesota, doctors had brought the news to Dad that he had a problem with his heart. Very few people could understand how difficult a blow that was to him. He was always on topside, but his heart was overwhelmed with grief at the thought that he might have to give up his ministry, his life. The news rocked Dad's world that day. For some reason Mom had not been able to go with him to the Mayo Clinic for this series of tests. Typically, they were always together, side-by-side, in almost every crisis.

That evening, his world would be rocked a second time; the phone would ring, and more bad news would come. Little Jack David, his five-year-old grandson, had died. From the Mayo Clinic bed, a hurting, broken-hearted man called his son. I was in the hospital when the call came. It was just a few minutes before the doctors would tell us they could not revive our son. I cannot remember a moment in my life more difficult than that moment. I cannot remember an event in my life more tragic and heart-wrenching than that moment. I could not believe that God would allow my sweet little boy to be taken.

Jack David was a very special child. I know every parent says that, but he really was. Everyone in our church knew it; everyone

The Passing Over of Dr. Jack Hyles

who came into contact with him knew it. What amazed me the most was that Jack David, at a very early age, was just like his grandpa. His personality was people-oriented. His personality was far more like my dad's personality than like mine. His eyes sparkled like his grandpa's eyes. He had his grandpa's same mischievous grin. When he walked into a room, he was a presence. He was not out of line, he was not obnoxious, he just loved life; and whenever he came into a room, he brought that love of life with him. Everyone felt Jack David was in a wonderful and positive way—just like his grandpa.

Jack David was born with an infection in his lungs. That infection put him in critical condition and caused him to be transferred to a special hospital, All Children's Hospital, in St. Petersburg, Florida. For several days we wondered if God was going to let us keep our little boy as he lay in critical condition. God did preserve his life, and while we were at his hospital bedside, we discovered that Jack David had a blood disease.

When our daughter Bethany was very young, she had several seizures and struggled with health problems. Thankfully, she grew out of them, but we sometimes wondered if something else was wrong that needed to be treated. So we took Bethany and Jack David to the University of South Florida Hospital for special tests. There we discovered that *both* of them had an unusual blood defect. The doctors discovered they were not able to eliminate all of the lactaid acid, a poison, out of their blood. The doctors were concerned about this situation because it could create other problems with their health. The syndrome was incurable. In a couple of weeks, we went back into the University Hospital to have both tested to prescribe some type of treatment. We went home, wondering what we were facing in the future.

Jack David

I remember talking to my dad and fearing that something would happen to my son. Bethany had seemed to outgrow some of her health problems, but as a baby, Jack David was still a critical health risk. Dad began to pray for both Bethany and Jack David.

For several weeks, we waited for the hospital to call and give us the results, but we never heard from them. One day Brenda took Jack David to the doctor for a regular check up. She told the doctor that we had not heard any results regarding the tests. The doctor called the University hospital to see if he could get those results. The doctor at the University of South Florida Hospital informed the doctor that the tests had come back negative, and there was no longer any sign of the blood disorder in either Bethany or Jack David. Brenda was so elated when she heard the news, she called me immediately to tell me. My first response was to say, "God has healed them."

We were thrilled. I could not believe our fears were eliminated, and our children were fine. When I called my dad on the phone to tell him what had happened, Dad, who was typically very stoic, not a real spooky talking kind of person, nor careless with his spiritual analysis, said, "God healed them. I had a feeling He would. I know God healed them."

It was very interesting that their blood disorder was discovered in a university hospital in Tampa. Dad died at the University of Chicago. But, there was something even more interesting.

In the final moments of Dad's death, the doctors discovered that one of the reasons why his blood pressure could not be stabilized was because his blood was filled with lactaid acid; it could not be flushed from his system. The nurse who worked on

The Passing Over of Dr. Jack Hyles

him throughout the night spent most of his time trying to reduce the lactaid acid count. He tried every possible way but was unable to succeed. Though Dad died with a heart problem, perhaps the main contributing factor that took my dad's life was the fact that they could not get the blood pressure up because of the lactaid acid levels in his blood. Thus, Dad died probably, indirectly, with the very thing with which his namesake, Jack David, was born.

Forgive me for thinking this, but I wonder if Dad took that disease from Jack David. My first thought was that maybe Jack inherited it from Dad. Upon further thought, I almost have to wonder if his grandfather prayed the disease to himself.

Jack David and my dad were buddies. A special bond existed between them that was very interesting. Whenever Jack was around Dad, he studied him. Jack would play when anyone else would preach, but he would sit perfectly still when he listened to his Grandpa. Dad fascinated Jack. He would talk about dreams he had of him and Grandpa walking on a beach together. We used to wonder what brought those ideas to Jack's mind. It was apparent that Jack had a special bond in his heart to Dad and that Dad had a special bond in his heart to Jack. I know he did not love Jack more than the rest of the grandchildren, but there was something unique between them. We saw it, and so did many others.

A couple of days after Jack David died, Dad came home from the Mayo Clinic. He and Mom flew into the Tampa airport to come to Pinellas Park for the funeral service. Dad did not speak at Jack's funeral though he did speak at the graveside service held in Indiana where Jack is buried. Dad just simply came as my dad and as Jack's grandpa. It had been one of the roughest weeks

Jack David

in his entire life. A couple from the church went to the airport to pick up Mom and Dad. All the rest of the family was waiting at the house because Dad wanted to get there just a few minutes before we had to leave for the church for the funeral.

When Mom and Dad arrived at the house, it was about 30 minutes before it was time to leave. They walked into the living room and sat down. One of the first things my dad said was, "Son, I want to tell you why Jack died." I was startled. As he told this story, he said, "When I was at Mayo Clinic, the night I found out that I had heart problems and the night Jack David died, I had fallen to sleep. In the middle of the night, God woke me up." He paused, "Son, you know I rarely take much stock in something like this, but I know this was of God. God woke me up and told me why Jack David died." I was stunned; but we were all sitting at the edges of our seats. He continued, "I was waiting until I got here so that I could tell you face to face. David, God took Jack David so that you would know how many people around this country love you. This was not punishment. God told me this was not punishment. This was not God looking down and chastening you. God merely wanted people around the country to have the opportunity to tell you how much they love you." I did not know what to say.

I find it interesting that for the first time in years, God had allowed me to feel loved again. I received literally hundreds, maybe thousands of messages, letters, notes, cards, and phone calls from people all over this nation telling me they loved me. Dad was positive about the reason, and somehow it gave me a little sense of peace. Isn't it also interesting that Dad was the one who knew why Jack David was taken, and he discovered it on the very night that he learned he had a heart problem?

The Passing Over of Dr. Jack Hyles

A month and a half later I went to Longview, Texas, to speak for Dr. Bob Gray. I was still grieving deeply. He had asked me to come to share some "rediscovered" Sunday school philosophies that I had been using in our church in Pinellas Park. All of these lessons were Dr. Jack Hyles' philosophies concerning the Sunday school.

I went to that first session to speak to several hundred pastors. As I stood in the back with my pastor, I said, "Brother Farris, I can't do this. My heart is in my throat, and I am so emotional."

He patted me on the back and said, "You can do it. God will help you." Dr. Bob Gray introduced me, and I walked to the front. I said the same words to the audience that I said to Brother Farris as I choked and as I stood in front of them. I know God gave me the grace that day to go on, and I spoke about the Sunday school. I would speak six more times on Dad's philosophies about the Sunday school. The response was unbelievable; more tapes were sold of that series on the Sunday school than any other sessions in the history of their soul-winning clinic. God began to do something unbelievable to revive the Sunday school movement in our Independent Baptist churches.

I received a letter shortly thereafter from a man who said, "When I saw you stand up to speak, I turned you off. I did not want to hear what you had to say. When you spoke about the loss of your son, and I saw your tears, I decided to hear you out. What you taught at the Soul-Winning Clinic has changed my ministry." I received many responses from people whose hearts were so tender and gracious to me.

Over a year later, in the summer of 2000, I was sitting in my

Jack David

parents' condominium, talking to Dad about the Sunday school. By this time, I had spoken in many churches and worked with many pastors, helping to revive and reorganize their Sunday schools. It was obvious that this Sunday school movement was sweeping across the country.

Allow me to say that I had no ambition for this and still do not. To be honest, at times I feel very reluctant; but every time I speak I tell about my son.

As I sat there that day, my dad said something that broke my heart yet challenged my soul. He said, "Jack David had to die so that the Sunday school could live." I thought about what he had said, and though the thought broke my heart in many ways, I knew that he was speaking the truth.

Consider this: The champion of Sunday schools has always been Jack Hyles. Perhaps the greatest builder in the history of the Sunday school was Jack Hyles. God reached down and took his grandson, Jack David Hyles, in order that his son might take the message of his grandpa to this country about the Sunday school. I am in awe when I think of the parallels and when I think how God worked in both of their lives.

On Dad's fortieth anniversary as pastor of First Baptist Church of Hammond, the church honored my parents with an elaborate banquet. Several thousand people came to honor Dad on the day before his birthday for his 40 years of ministry. We stayed at the Sheraton Hotel in downtown Chicago. Mom and Dad had been given a room in the presidential suite.

We had decided that the next morning we were going to have a birthday breakfast for Dad. After that, we would have to catch a plane and come back to Florida. My family and I tried to think of what we could give Dad as a gift. We thought and

The Passing Over of Dr. Jack Hyles

thought and thought. When we were in the gift shop in the Sheraton Hotel, we saw a picture frame that had a soccer ball, a basketball, a football and a baseball on top of it—one of those little boy kinds of frames. In my Bible I had a picture of my dad and Jack David on a boat ride we had taken on Lake Michigan the summer before Jack David died. Grandpa and Jack David had posed together for this special picture. We trimmed the picture a little, placed it in the frame, and wrapped it.

The next morning, when Dad was opening gifts, he opened ours; he spoke to me in many words he had never before expressed. The minute he looked at that picture, he began to weep; and we all sat around the table together and wept. It was then that the family knew just how deeply my dad had loved Jack David and how deeply it had hurt him to lose him. Yes, a special bond existed between Jack David and Grandpa, but there was also a special bond between Grandpa and Jack David.

Jack David and his grandpa

As we stood around Dad's bed knowing that any moment he would go to Heaven, I thought about Jack David. I leaned over to my wife and whispered in her ear, "Somehow I think Jack David is jumping up and down in Heaven saying, 'Hurry up,

Jack David

Grandpa! Hurry up, Grandpa! Come on, Grandpa! I am waiting for you! Hurry up, Grandpa! Come Home, Grandpa!' "

Of course, there were many other loved ones waiting for him on the Other Side, and I know that Jack David was not the only one whom Dad wanted to see. Somehow in my own my mind, I cannot help but think that Jack Hyles has a shadow. The shadow of a little boy, his namesake, Jack David, follows him everywhere he goes and watches his every move—just like he did on earth.

CHAPTER

17

Dad's Office

"I thank my God upon every remembrance of you."
(Philippians 1:3)

T WAS AN EERIE feeling when we first walked into his office. It was the first time that I had been there since Dad died. Mom had stopped several times after services just to spend a few minutes in there; for her it was a place of refuge as well as a place to ponder and reflect on Dad. It was as though she still had a place to go where he still "belonged." But now we were about to embark upon the task which we, at first, had wished to avoid but which now had to be done.

We knew that Dad's office would be a very important part of the aftermath of his death. We realized that, in the course of time, another man, a new pastor, would occupy that office. We would eventually have to go in and begin the very difficult process of removing Dad's things. We first scheduled time to

Dad's Office

meet in mid-March in Hammond to begin cleaning out his office. However, the machinery of the pulpit committee moved much more rapidly than we had anticipated, and we were forced to make a quick decision to begin this process much earlier. Dad had been gone less then three weeks on the day we first entered to begin our work. It was perhaps too quick for us. We had to take advantage of the opportunity that was afforded to us. At 12:30, on Monday, February 26, just 20 days after Dad's death, Mom, Brenda, and I began to go through Dad's things. I felt that the experience was such that I would be amiss not to include it in a chapter in this book, so I am going to share some of the experiences of the two days we gave to cleaning out Dad's office.

Dad's office was not a showpiece. It was not a place of pretentiousness. Dad's office was his workshop, his tool shop, his mechanical garage—the place where he worked. It was not a place that was designed to impress but rather to accomplish. It was always surprising to everyone that Dad did not have a fancier office, but Dad's office meant nothing to him in the sense of an image. He was not establishing an image; he was producing a product. Dad designed an office, not to make himself feel important, but to produce sermons. When we began the process of cleaning out his office, we discovered exactly where his priorities were.

The first word that came to our minds when we began to go through his office was "packrat." In many ways, it appeared that he was a packrat. I guess to a degree, I would have to admit that it was true. However, I think it is more than that; I believe Dad kept things that he thought he might use again in his trade. Let me explain: when a man has a workshop, he may save a nut, a bolt, a screw, a nail or even a tool that he seldom uses just

The Passing Over of Dr. Jack Hyles

because he might use it again some day. He might save items that to some might seem worthless, but he foresaw the possibility of their use. That is exactly what Dad did with his office. Many of the items that were stashed away in his office were things he had put there for a potential use in the future. His cabinets and his drawers were jammed and packed with books, notes, sermons, and ideas—more than anyone could imagine. His office was filled with cabinet space and drawer space; each and every one of those cabinets and drawers was packed and jammed. Even behind his desk, stacks and stacks of books he had used at one time were piled. This leads me to another thought about Dad.

Dad did not collect books; in fact, Dad did not even really read books. He used his books as tools. He tore pages out of them, and he wrote in them. Entire chapters of books would be torn out, and he would take them with him somewhere because of an idea that he had gotten. To Dad, books were merely a tool. He used an incredible variety of books to find sermon ideas. Dad did not read books to decide what he believed; sometimes he read books to look for ideas from people who believed totally differently than he did. He knew what he believed; thus he read books not to discover truth but to discover an idea to present the truth he already believed. That was one of the most fascinating things about Dad.

Forgive me, but there were authors in his office that Dad was diametrically opposed to in his beliefs; yet in their books we spotted underlined pages of passages. Notes were jotted in the margins. Sometimes pages were torn out because of an idea, and we would find those pages elsewhere in the office. In nearly every case, it was not some truth that he was trying to find, but rather an idea that he could use to present the truths that he

Dad's Office

embraced. Thousands of books were packed in those cabinets and drawers with notes written in many, many of them for ideas for sermons that he one day planned to preach.

His office revealed to me that Dad never really got over who he was. Newspaper clippings from preaching engagements from many, many years ago up until just a few weeks before his Homegoing were in his office. We came across flyers and promotional items that told about his preaching engagements— why would he save them?! Why would some flyer from a little church mean something to him? I believe Dad never got over the fact that people wanted *him* to come and preach. He never got used to the idea that people wanted him. He never became a big shot; he remained a simple man who was enamored by the simple thought that people wanted him to preach for them. He saved everything, hoping maybe one day to go back and relive it all again—obviously, that would never be.

Some of the amazing array of items that we found in his office surprised us. Ties, old shoes, peanut butter that was so old it had liquefied, vitamins ten years past their expiration date, and a box of golf balls were some discoveries. We found memos from many, many years ago, and photo albums from staff events from 25 years before and sometimes even older than that! Some newspaper clippings were 35 years old. How amazing to go through cabinets and drawers and find 42 years of a man's life stuffed into each one!

Perhaps the most incredible thing that I came away with concerning my dad was this: Dad lived, breathed, walked, and talked in sermon preparation. The evidences of his study were everywhere. Sermon outlines were written on every imaginary type of paper and stuffed in every cabinet, every drawer, every

The Passing Over of Dr. Jack Hyles

book, and every Bible. Everywhere a person turned were sermons—not just complete sermons, but sermon ideas written on 3x5 cards, written on pages torn out of books, and written on napkins. Sermon ideas were everywhere, and sermon outlines were everywhere. Literally thousands of sermons were in his office—many of which he never preached. When I talked to Mom, she told me that Dad spent every waking free moment studying and preparing sermons. Dad loved his people so much. It was not just that Dad loved to preach, but he saw preaching for what it was; a way to touch lives and a way to meet the needs. I suppose the best the way to describe it would be as follows: A person who is a cook writes down every recipe, every possible combination of ingredients, has recipe book after recipe book underlined, marked, and filled with clippings from newspapers and magazines and even more recipes. That is exactly what Dad did about sermons. These were his "recipes," and they were everywhere. His entire office was a workshop where he turned out sermons.

On that first day that we were in Dad's office, we had to go through each and every cabinet, trying to separate and organize all of the contents. Mom was a little overwhelmed by it all; things had moved so fast for her. Most of the time she sat and watched and supervised. One of the interesting comments Mom kept saying to us about Dad was, "Bless his heart, he was so busy. He just did not have time to do what we are doing today." Or she would say, "Bless his heart. Dad had so much to do he did not have time to get organized." At another time, she also said, "Dad is looking down from Heaven right now and laughing at us because we are having to do what he did not have time to do." We laughed and reminisced a lot that day. Though it was a

Dad's Office

very emotionally draining day, a certain amount of sweetness seeped through of having the opportunity to get a closeup look at Dad's workshop.

We started at 12:30 and worked until finally the dust filled our lungs. We were filthy and a bit tired. Mom decided it was time to have dinner. We drove to a restaurant and had a nice meal together. Jack and Cindy's son Kenny wanted to see Grandpa's office before it was empty, so we decided to go back to the office for a little while in the evening. Brenda and I, Jack and Cindy, and Kenny decided to meet there. When I arrived at the church, I was trying to find a security guard to let me in the building. I walked around to the dumpster where we had dumped a lot of what we had considered "trash." A car was parked there, and the back seat was jammed with "trash" that some security guards had pulled out of the dumpster.

At that point, I believe that I truly realized how valuable everything in his office really was. Please, understand me, my mom felt a tremendous sense of pride about not wanting to barter off Dad's things. It bothered her. Again, as it was with the funeral, Mom felt a sense of dignity and a sense of not wanting to cheapen Dad's death. But I really saw that night that an old pair of 20-year-ago shoes had significance to someone simply because they were Jack Hyles' shoes. What a strange phenomenon for me to comprehend! I valued so many things in his office. I valued the books, the Bibles, the plaques, the notes, the memos, the files, but to some people a 3x5 card with a note jotted on it would have been of great value. This caused us on the second day to be a little more aware about being careful with what we were finding.

That evening we spent about an hour and a half going

The Passing Over of Dr. Jack Hyles

through more things in Dad's office until finally we were exhausted. Around 9:00, we wrapped up our first day. The office was a mess. We had gone through probably half of the cabinets and drawers, but we still had a lot of work looming ahead of us for the next day.

Mom was worn out emotionally that first day. I guess I did not realize just how taxing the job would be on her. I knew it was on me, but it was even more difficult for her to endure. So the next day, Mom spent about an hour with us in the office, and we basically spent the remainder of the day by ourselves going through things. We reached a point where we had to start boxing up some books to decide later what to do with them. As we sorted through things, we had several piles. Jack and Cindy had chosen things that they wanted to keep for themselves and their family. Brenda and I had a pile of things that we wanted to keep for our family. We set aside many items for Mom. Still another assortment was put aside that consisted of things that were given to Dad by people who were still in the ministries of First Baptist Church, such as plaques and books signed by members of the church. We did our best to filter through these things and set them aside to be returned to those who had given them to him as a memento to keep. Each time we returned something to a person, we received the same reaction; the person would weep and say how thankful he was.

Let me share with you one sweet story. We were going through things that Dad had piled in a closet by his bathroom. I found a homemade shelf that looked like something perhaps made by a teenage boy in a wood shop class. I noticed a little plaque was attached to it. Roy and JoJo Moffitt's son, Roy Moffitt, Jr., had given it to Dad. He had obviously made it in his

Dad's Office

wood shop class. I set it aside and thought, "Well, if I see Brother Roy I will give this to him." This was on Monday.

Tuesday, I saw Brother Moffitt and said, "Brother Moffitt, I have something for you." I went into the office and got the shelf, and brought it out, and handed it to him.

He said, "Brother Dave, my son asked me last night, 'I wonder what they are going to do with the shelf I made Brother Hyles.'"

Our returning that shelf was very meaningful to him. A few days later, when I was at my mother's house, the phone rang. It was Roy Moffitt Jr. Through tears, he thanked me for returning that shelf. That is just an example of how sweet it was to see the depth of feelings people had toward my dad. How precious those items were to the giver and receiver.

I also found several items given to my dad by Maxine Jeffries and the Deaf Department. The first time I found something, left the office, and gave it to her, she too broke down and wept because it was deeply meaningful to her to receive it.

Finally, late Tuesday afternoon, we were finished. About 5:00 Tuesday afternoon, everyone had left. Brenda and I were left alone in the office; as we began to get things together to leave, I remember the deep emotional feelings that I had.

I went back into Dad's office, sat down, and began to weep. I realized that now every cabinet was empty, every drawer was empty, the closet was cleaned out, and every book was packed. As I looked at his office, I began to realize that 42 years of my dad's life had just been cleaned out of this room, and my heart broke. I think that was one of the most difficult moments in the aftermath of Dad's death. I remember how difficult it was to walk out of his office knowing, just as we had known that he

The Passing Over of Dr. Jack Hyles

would never walk back in the pulpit of First Baptist, he would never walk back into this office. This empty office was another ending.

There are so many stories about his office that I wish I could share. The experience was precious and one that I will never forget. His old briefcases, his old Bibles, all of his sermon notes, every plaque, every little note and memo were very dear and precious to us.

We made several decisions. Whatever books we did not want or were not being returned to someone would be inventoried and placed in storage at the college until we could decide later what to do with them. All of his sermon notes and all of his preaching Bibles were boxed and placed in safekeeping for the possibility of later doing some-

A look into Dad's life

thing special with these. We knew we would not give away any of these. We thought we would try to share these with the world perhaps later in a library-type setting. All of these very precious things were dealt with very carefully for we knew that each of

Dad's Office

them had great intrinsic value.

A part of me wanted to give everyone who loved him a piece of him, but I knew that was impossible. I knew that every member of the church could not have something out of his office. I knew that we could disperse pieces of his things everywhere, and each person could enjoy a small little token, but we all felt that it was important to do the best we could to collectively keep his things together. We believe that possibly a place could be designated where these belongings could be, more than just looked at, even used to help future Christians in some way.

I believe it is important to take a moment and discuss what we did not find in Dad's office. I do not know but what some of the sweetest thoughts I have about this difficult task was what I did not find. I did not expect to find these things. Quite frankly, I knew I would not, but indulge me a moment because I heard my dad attacked and accused by so many people, and I cannot help but gloat a bit about what was not there.

Not one item of indiscretion was found in Dad's office, not one. Not one book, not one publication, not one file, not one card, not one letter, not one thing in his office was indiscreet. Imagine what it would be like if someone went through your closets and your drawers and you had to explain why certain items were there. Dad had nothing to explain because nothing was there that needed explaining.

Someone once said that Dad had gold bars hidden in his office. I am sad to tell you that four silver Canadian dollars is all that we found. I wish I could say that we found the gold bars. I certainly would have been happy. The truth of the matter is, what I found in Dad's office was the same Jack Hyles that was

The Passing Over of Dr. Jack Hyles

found behind the pulpit—transparent, real, honest, and right. Dad's office was a testimony to his life. Not one time did we find a single thing that did not exemplify his entire ministry.

I came away from this experience with many precious things in hand. I drove back to Florida with a car loaded down with very important and precious memories including a briefcase, a pair of glasses, Bibles, books, notes, files, and pictures. I had many, many precious items that I will cherish, but I came back to Florida with more than just possessions. I came back with a greater appreciation and understanding of my dad. I returned to Florida having experienced two days in the workshop of a master craftsman. I got to see how he worked, what he lived for, and what he was all about. I got to feel what really consumed him; his people consumed him. For every breathing moment of his life, he was searching for something to give his people. Every moment that he had he was doing his best to meet the needs of those God had given to his care. No, his office was never fancy. Yes, he seemed to have been somewhat of a packrat, but what he really was, was a man who loved his people. He, a master craftsman, used his office as a workshop, if you please, to prepare that which would help his people and make them strong.

18

Life Goes On

"And there are also many other things which Jesus did,
the which, if they should be written every one,
I suppose that even the world itself could not contain
the books that should be written."
(John 21:25)

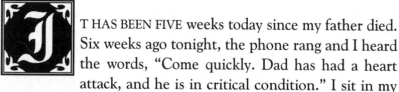T HAS BEEN FIVE weeks today since my father died. Six weeks ago tonight, the phone rang and I heard the words, "Come quickly. Dad has had a heart attack, and he is in critical condition." I sit in my office in Pinellas Park, Florida, writing this final chapter. In Indiana, a widow grieves over the loss of her husband. Day by day, she faces new experiences that bring to mind the finality of his death.

Throughout the Hammond area, a church continues to grieve the loss of their beloved pastor. Throughout the country, a nation of Christians continue to grieve at the loss of their

The Passing Over of Dr. Jack Hyles

leader and hero. I have talked to Mom almost every day since Dad's death. I think the one statement that Mom said that sums up the conclusion of this story are these words: "David, it is hard to believe, and it is hard to accept; but for most people, life just goes on."

It is true; life does go on. As of the writing of this chapter, there is now a new pastor of First Baptist Church. As of the writing of this chapter, most people have stopped weeping. Though they are still grieving, they have gone on with their lives and returned to some sense of normalcy. Even family members, in many cases, are now back to life as it was before Dad died, although our grief is still as great and deep. Mom goes on with her mourning for she has lost the love of her life and her best friend. Her heart aches, and life will never be the same for her; she knows that, as do we all. I am now the owner of Dad's car, having bought it from Mom. His office has been cleaned, his name is no longer the name that will appear on the letterhead of First Baptist Church or Hyles-Anderson College. So much has changed in such a short time; however, it seems like life just goes on.

But this I will say, there is a man on the Other Shore waiting for us there. He is now a part of the great cloud of witnesses; his name is Dr. Jack Hyles, my dad. And though life goes on, he made a difference in thousands and tens of thousands, yea, even hundreds of thousands of lives. For those whom he touched, some for many years, some for just a few moments, life will never be the quite same. Perhaps John, dad's nurse, summed it up best for all of us. As Dad was being rolled into surgery to begin his journey to the Other Shore, John simply said, "That is a good man."

*"I shall not die, but live,
and declare the works of the LORD."*
(Psalms 118:17)

Appendix 1

HE FOLLOWING PAGES CONTAIN a sampling of the many articles that appeared in various newspapers.

Rev. Jack Hyles; led bus ministry
February 9, 2001
by James Janega
Chicago Tribune Staff Writer

Every Sunday morning since the 1960s, the salvation motorcade has issued forth: hundreds of buses scouring the Chicago area as far north as Waukegan to bring the faithful—some of them on-the-spot converts—to the First Baptist Church and Sunday school in Hammond, Ind.

Each week, tens of thousands flocked to First Baptist services led by Rev. Jack Hyles, the fundamentalist and often controversial Baptist preacher who put his church, and the concept of the bus ministry, on the religious map. Rev. Hyles, 74, who used the buses to create the first megachurch in the Chicago area, and in the process led other inner-city churches to

Appendixes

do the same in the 1960s and '70s, died Tuesday, Feb. 6, in University of Chicago Hospitals, where he was undergoing open-heart surgery.

"Dr. Hyles will be remembered as a leader in evangelism through the local church," said Rev. Jerry Falwell, televangelist and chancellor of Liberty University. "He inspired me as a young pastor to win others to Christ through Sunday school, the pulpit and personal witnessing. He made a great contribution to the cause of Christ."

With homespun humor and uncompromising religious fervor, Rev. Hyles enunciated a clear and deeply conservative vision of how his church should be run. Smoking and drinking were out, of course, as were dancing and hand-holding for unmarried couples.

But it was his literal interpretation of the Bible that often put him at odds even with other fundamental Baptists. During his career, he split with both the Southern Baptist Convention and the American Baptist Convention.

When he first came to Hammond in 1959, the preacher who had packed new converts into his former Texas congregations sent liberal Northern churchgoers fleeing. But he quickly turned things around, first by going door to door for new followers, then by sending the buses when distances got too far.

Some 20,000 people now attend church services and Sunday school each week at First Baptist, which also serves as the parent congregation for the Hammond Baptist Schools, Hyles-Anderson College and the Hyles Publications religious press.

"In many ways, he was larger than life," said Hammond Mayor Duane Dedelow Jr. "He had a tremendous following at his church, but when other people were moving out of

The Passing Over of Dr. Jack Hyles

downtown Hammond, the reverend decided to stay. Many of his congregation lived in Hammond, so I would say he had a very important impact here."

Raised in a poverty-stricken area of Dallas, Rev. Hyles often described a less-than-ideal childhood with distant parents. Drafted into the Army after high school, he was married during that period to the former Beverly Slaughter.

He graduated from the East Texas Baptist College after the war and set out preaching in small Texas congregations, all of which soon got large.

"His churches always grew," said Wendell Evans, president of Hyles-Anderson College. "He was very godly, but very practical."

The largest of those 1950s congregations was the Miller Road Baptist Church in Garland, Texas, which grew from a membership of 44 to 4,000. Though his success initially gained him wide admiration among Southern Baptists, Rev. Hyles later split from the group over theological differences, opting instead to run Miller Road as an independent preacher.

"Rev. Hyles hated the word 'minister,'" Evans said, "finding it too 'sissified.'"

After being invited to head the then-high society First Baptist Church in Hammond, he presided over a mass defection of its tonier membership that diminished its 700-person congregation by a third. Soon afterward, he led the church out of the American Baptist Conference and initiated his extensive bus ministry.

The author of 49 self-published treatises on theology with a circulation of more than 14 million copies, Rev. Hyles founded the Hammond Baptist Schools in 1970 and Hyles-Anderson

Appendixes

College in Crown Point, Ind., in 1972.

In addition to his wife, he is survived by daughters Becky Smith, Linda Murphrey and Cindy Schaap; a son, David; a sister, Earlyne Stephens; 11 grandchildren; and four great-grand-children.

Visitation for Rev. Hyles will be held from 10 A.M. to 6:30 P.M. Friday in the First Baptist Church, 523 Sibley St., followed by a 7 P.M. memorial serve in the church for non-church members. A funeral service for church members will be at 10 A.M. Saturday in the church.

[Obituary reprinted by permission of the Chicago Tribune February 9, 2001]

Longtime Spiritual Leader, the Rev. Hyles, dead at 74
Wednesday, February 7, 2001
By Debra Gruszecki and Lu Ann Franklin
Times Staff Reporters

Pastor at First Baptist Church of Hammond called an unselfish mentor

HAMMOND - The Rev. Jack Hyles did the unthinkable Tuesday. The man who, for more than 40 years was a driving force spiritually and educationally to an uncountable tally of followers in Northwest Indiana and the country, died Tuesday morning at the University of Chicago Hospitals.

The Passing Over of Dr. Jack Hyles

His death was a stunning blow, as the 74-year-old pastor of First Baptist Church of Hammond and founder of Hyles-Anderson College led his congregation with all the zeal of a freshly starched, spit-shine polished graduate of Bible School.

"I don't have words to express how sad I feel today," Amber Kent, a senior at Hammond Baptist High School, said as she headed to the parish office in downtown Hammond. "We'd been praying, and singing for an hour before we got the news of Brothers Hyles' death."

When students were told about the fatal complications of Hyles' bypass surgery in Chicago, "the whole school lost it," Kent said.

Tears streamed down the faces of teachers and students as they huddled in classrooms, and worries ran deep, even after school had been dismissed. Students at Hyles-Anderson College in Schererville were in mourning too, according to President Wendell Evans.

"He was our motivator and our leader," said Evans, who has served as college president since the school's founding by Hyles in 1972. "He helped me a lot in learning the principles of leadership, administration and counseling. He was very unselfish in helping people, including our students."

Hyles, who was born in Italy, Texas, and grew up in a poverty-stricken area of Dallas, attended Southwest Baptist Seminary after graduating from East Texas Baptist College. Before coming to Hammond in 1959, Hyles led the Miller Road Baptist Church in Garland, Texas, for about six years, from a membership of 44 people to 4,000.

By May 1965, Hyles' sermons from the pulpit had become so popular that they found their way into books, such as *Kisses of*

Appendixes

Calvary, which contains an introduction from Hyles' mother: The Jack she saw grow from boyhood to manhood, was a person who gave Christ first place in his life, she wrote, and always had a great love and burden for lost souls.

Those lost souls, as Hyles put it, found their way onto buses that fanned out across Northwest Indiana and the low-income areas of Chicago, to bring a following to Hammond on Sundays and spread the word about the simplicity of salvation.

The 1970s brought new Baptist-run schools to the area and Hyles-Anderson College. The decade also brought a new First Baptist Church auditorium addition to 523 Sibley St. and a national Christian Life Magazine report claiming that the church operated one of the largest Sunday schools in the nation, and possibly the world.

Annual pastors schools were held in the spring, as were youth conferences, which drew thousands to the area and even promoted marquee "Welcome" signs from merchants along the traffic route between the college and the church. The college also grew in enrollment and influence over the years, as its annual school roster has grown from 300 to 1,800 students from across the nation.

"He had several thousand pastors who looked to him as a mentor, even before this college was founded," Evans said. "They have (since) sent students here."

Hyles was especially good at attracting students, Evans said.

One such student, Phil Merhalski, director of economic development for the city of Hammond, said Hyles was the matchmaker in his marriage to his wife, Gail, in 1977. The pastor's impact on their lives, and the city, was "so encompassing," Merhalski said.

The Passing Over of Dr. Jack Hyles

Merhalski added Hyles put buildings to new uses in downtown Hammond, setting up various ministries that included outreach programs for Spanish-speaking people and the homeless.

"He was instrumental in stabilizing the downtown and the city itself," said Merhalski, who has been a member of the church since 1973. "He believed in people and saw things (in individuals) other people didn't. He was a caring, loving man."

Hammond Mayor Duane Dedelow Jr. said he was saddened by Hyles' death.

"His contributions over the years to the city of Hammond have been great, both spiritually, and through his commitment to stay in the downtown area when others were leaving. He has forever left his imprint on the city," said Dedelow, who met Hyles when he first entered politics in 1991.

The city's Redevelopment Commission, in fact, was talking about a plan to add a Youth Center to the downtown cluster of ministries, at about 9:43 A.M., the time Hyles died. It almost seemed a bit ironic, said commission member Mark Rincon, and seems to be a sign that Hyles' ministry will continue.

Shelton Smith, president and editor of Sword of the Lord, a religious publication based in Tennessee, said Hyles was a major player in a worldwide, fundamental movement over the last 45 years, and as such, has had a "major impact on tens of thousands of people around the country and the world."

Hyles, who served on the board of directors with Sword of the Lord and was a guest speaker for Sword-sponsored conferences, has also had his share of personal-and-ministry-related controversy.

When controversy flared, many of Hyles' followers grew

Appendixes

more adamant about his ministry and committed to it. Hyles also deflected criticism by saying that when one has a church of more than 10,000, it is inevitable that some members may find their way into the news.

Smith refused to talk about Hyles' controversies.

"This is a time to think about the wonderful things he has done," Smith said. "The big thing that he has kept the focus on is winning people to Christ. A lot of people have been motivated by Dr. Hyles to invest their lives in seeking out others and attempting to bring them to Christ."

Hyles, who at times was called flamboyant and at times, a bit shy, had a "dynamic about his personality that was influential on everybody he came in contact with," Smith said. "I would say that the people who knew him well would describe him as a gentle and compassionate man who cared very deeply about the people around him."

FUNERAL ARRANGEMENTS

The viewing of the Rev. Jack Hyles' body will be held in the First Baptist Church of Hammond auditorium, 523 Sibley St., from 10 A.M. to 6:30 P.M. Friday. A memorial service for all out-of-town guests and friends, all non-First Baptist Church members will begin at 7 P.M. Friday.

After the memorial service, the viewing will continue throughout the night until 9:30 A.M. Saturday. A funeral service for First Baptist Church members, including the church's college students, will be held at 10 A.M. Saturday. A private graveside service for family members only will follow.

The Passing Over of Dr. Jack Hyles

THE LIFE OF JACK HYLES

September 1959: The Rev. Jack Hyles is named pastor of First Baptist Church, moving to Hammond from a small 44-member church in Garland, Texas, to begin a thriving, fundamental New Testament Baptist church at 523 Sibley.

March 1963: The first First Baptist church Pastors' School, a program that continues to draw pastors from across the nation, is held in Hammond. The first pastor training program attracted 65 preachers, according to news clips. Twelve years later, attendance was reported to be 3,100.

September 1970: First Baptist Church opens a high school in Lake Ridge School, Calumet Township, and begins to operate a grade school at 700 Sibley St.

September 1972: A full schedule of classes begins at Hyles-Anderson College, which sprang up in Schererville on the grounds of the former Capuchin Seminary of St. Mary. College officials claim Hyles-Anderson to have the largest first-year enrollment of any independent Bible college in the history of America.

February 1975: A new $2 million First Baptist Church auditorium is dedicated at 523 Sibley St. and described as one of the largest meeting centers in the Calumet Region.

March 1975: *Christian Life* Magazine reports that First Baptist Church operates one of the largest Sunday schools in the nation, and possibly the world, and has an average weekly attendance of 7,837 to 10,000. During a 10-week bus ministry effort church members reported that as many as 15,000 people rode the church's 200 buses each Sunday.

June 1977: First Baptist Church purchased the Duckles Bible Camp in Macoupin County, Ill.

Appendixes

June 2, 1977: Hyles-Anderson College reports its largest graduating class, with more than 160 graduates, and gets permission to begin the first of many expansions on campus: construction of a 2,000-seat chapel where the Rev. Jack Hyles preached weekly.

July 1993: Thousands participate in the National Church Bus Ministry Parade in Downtown Chicago, an event organized to counteract media criticism of First Baptist Church of Hammond and its bus ministry. The parade drew 150 multicolored buses and 75 floats, and comments from pastors across the nation about the merits of the Hammond-based ministry that has helped many and has transported between 7,000 and 10,000 riders to Sunday school in Hammond each week for decades. Many of the riders are minority children from low-income areas of Chicago.

The Passing Over of Dr. Jack Hyles

'Don't let what I taught you die'

Thousands Gather to Pay Last Respects to the Rev. Hyles

Saturday, February 10, 2001
By Debra Gruszecki
Times Staff Writer

Thousands of Baptists got "Blessed Assurance" in a memorial service at First Baptist Church of Hammond on Friday that the ministry of the Rev. Jack Frasure Hyles will go on.

Hyles, who began preaching at the age of 19 and pastored for 54 years, left a legacy of Bible-thumping, soul-winning people behind.

"Our loss is Heaven's gain," said Russell Anderson, a cofounder of Hyles-Anderson College.

Anderson recalled the preacher telling him, "When it comes my time for leaving, there will be no grieving."

The mood though somber, was upbeat.

It was also compelling.

Some of the people closest to Hyles stepped up to the podium, including son David and Hyles' wife, Beverly.

Beverly, before drawing a standing ovation, told those in the audience that the newspapers said her husband died Tuesday of complications from heart bypass surgery.

"I believe he died of a tired heart, a weary heart," she said. "He loved people, serving people, helping people, and when he had to say, 'no,' because he did not have the strength or the time, it hurt him deeply."

Appendixes

Before Beverly turned the nearly two-hour service over to others, she advised mourners to use what they'd learned from her husband and apply it to their lives.

"You did not learn from Jack Hyles," she said. "You learned it from God because he walked with God."

Hyles' son, David, said his father lived his life a little above the clouds.

The man who became pastor of First Baptist Church in August, 1959, always had an optimistic view on life and its challenges and controversies, David Hyles said.

The clouds were his carpet and the sky his footstool, David said.

"When he visited a church, he wouldn't come to cry with you, but to lift you," he said.

Speaker Jeff Owens said Hyles did not act like a big shot. He was not arrogant, and never talked down to people.

"He put the jelly on the bottom of the shelf," so young people could reach it. "And a million children reached it."

Owens said Hyles' contributions were many, and he never lost faith in humanity, regardless of how hard critics attacked.

"He taught us that the ground is level at the foot of the cross," Owens said.

Ray Young wondered how many marriages and ministries Hyles saved.

"I wonder how many alcoholics he reclaimed," Young said. "Only eternity will tell how many people he touched."

With that, and a few psalms—and details about Hyles' humble approach to a church that increased in property value from $7,000 to over $70 million and in size from 44 to over 100,000 people, there came a voice.

The Passing Over of Dr. Jack Hyles

It was Hyles' voice—on tape—telling all riveted in their chairs that he is just a voice.

"And when I'm gone, and my voice is silent, and you come to see me, don't let what I taught you die."

"I believe he died of a tired heart, a weary heart. He loved people, serving people, helping people, and when he had to say, 'no,' because he did not have the strength or the time, it hurt him deeply."

–Beverly Hyles,
the Rev. Hyles' wife

Mourners Brave Bad Weather, Travel Long Distances to Say Goodbye
Saturday, February 10, 2001
By Debra Gruszecki
Times Staff Writer

The Rev. Jack Hyles, a common man who drove a common car, ate Reeses' Peanut Butter Cups and supped on Whopper Jrs. minus mayonnaise, drew no common crowd Friday for the first of two memorial services.

Hyles, who died Tuesday, lay in repose as thousands streamed past his casket and an untold number of bouquets that friends and family had sent to First Baptist Church of Hammond to accompany him.

Local residents came to pay their respects. Hyles-Anderson

Appendixes

College students and faculty members were present, some staking out seats for the 7 P.M. service as early as 10 A.M. to honor a man who had been their preacher since 1959.

There were reports that some had been waiting in the rain for hours before the doors opened, so they could be first to step inside the church auditorium at 523 Sibley St., which they liken to home.

Longtime members such as Barbara Mock, whose grandfather, James Beilby, helped found First Baptist Church, couldn't stay away. Nor could a missionary who flew in from the Philippines, nor John Kolentas, who drove in from New York.

Becky Towne, a 1980 Hammond Baptist graduate, flew in for the funeral services from Pasco, Wash. Clint and Candy Miller flew in from San Diego with their family, and as one roamed from pew to pew, it became obvious rather quickly that they were among countless others.

What was it that drew people to Hyles?

"Everybody here can say something, but honestly, what he taught us from the Bible gave me the life and the family and the ministry that I have," reflected Hyles-Anderson College instructor, Bob Hooker, as tears welled up in his eyes as he paused to carefully collect his words.

Hooker said he was saved in 1975, while attending Memphis State University and came to Indiana about two years after hearing Hyles preach. "He taught us how to treat each other as family, how to rear our kids, how to live for God and how to love people," he said.

He taught, said Clint Miller, by example. Miller, who is pastor of North County Baptist Church in Escondido, Calif., called Hyles his mentor, counselor, friend and pastor.

The Passing Over of Dr. Jack Hyles

"If it weren't for Jack Hyles," Miller's wife, Candy, said, "we wouldn't have a ministry."

Hyles called him to preach. And when Miller bid on a church, but could not scrape together enough money for an escrow payment to buy the building, he got an envelope in the mail. "I opened it up, and it held a $10,000 certified check and the note, 'To my friend, Clint Miller. I love you.' " Miller said. "that was in November 1995."

Miller said his church membership since has grown from a handful of members to 1,000 and it is home to the Miller Band, which recently put five songs on the gospel music charts, among them, "Unclouded Day."

If that wasn't enough, Hyles also sent over Miller's first church bus—a teal bus with a new engine that Hyles said he revved up for soul-winning in Escondido. And there was a black suit that Hyles gave to Miller when he flew in two years ago to get an honorary doctoral degree.

Miller stroked the lapel, and said, "I'm wearing it today."

Appendixes

Pastor's 'Family' Says Goodbye
Thousands of Mourners Attend
the Funeral of the Rev. Jack Hyles

Sunday, February 11, 2001
By Deborah Laverty
Times Staff Writer

The Rev. Jack Hyles built a ministry with more than 100,000 followers during his 41 years at First Baptist Church of Hammond.

Yet members, including Daniel Pina, who came to pay their last respects to Hyles at his funeral Saturday, recalled the way the charismatic, loving man singled them out as if they were each the most important person in the world.

Hyles, 74, died Tuesday morning at the University of Chicago Hospitals.

"He treated us like we were his family. He led such a great number of people in his church, yet he treated each person like an individual. He loved each person," recalled Pina.

Pina, along with his father and mother, Domingo Pina Jr. and Yolanda Pina, sat in balcony seats enabling them to look down at the service below.

"What I remember most about him was his compassion, his caring," said Gerardo Pineda of Chicago, a member of the church since 1988.

"He touched many lives," said Amanda Harris, who handed out programs and booklets detailing Hyles' life to those attending the funeral.

Every seat in the church, which has a capacity of 7,000, was

The Passing Over of Dr. Jack Hyles

filled, with some members opting to sit on metal folding chairs set up temporarily in the aisles.

Before the service, which started at 10 A.M., hundred of Hyles' followers lined up to file silently past his open casket to say goodbye.

The casket, surrounded by dozens of floral arrangements and covered with an American flag, was closed when the service started.

Following the singing of "Blessed Assurance" by the congregation, Eddie Lapina, youth minister, spoke briefly about his friend.

"The service today is for the hometown folks. It's a good time but a sad time," Lapina said.

Hyles' son, David, said the passing of his father was a troubling time for the family.

"We were filled with confusion as to what to do next," he said.

Hyles said the family yearned for the earlier privacy it had been able to experience in the hospital while his father was alive but knew it had to move on.

"It was difficult to accept that we weren't the only family...There is his church family and his family across the nation. Last night at the memorial service we had people here from all over the nation. This service is for the church family," he said.

Jack Hyles' wife, Beverly, spoke of the love her husband had for his large congregation and the loss to all.

"He truly loved you...I lost my best friend, my sweetheart, but we all lost our pastor...He loved being our pastor...He loved being a pastor. It was his favorite word," Beverly Hyles said.

Appendixes

Lapina closed the service, speaking of the national and worldwide impact Hyles had. Hyles trained more than 1,000 pastors and missionaries serving in the United States and in foreign lands.

"Dr. Jack Hyles' voice was heard all over the world. He was a preacher of preachers. He set the standard," Lapina said.

He also spoke of the wide variety of those in Hyles' large flock, including those who were homeless and those with handicaps.

"He looked for those who no one else looked for," Lapina said.

He said Hyles, despite his worldwide influence, never forgot his large family of church members in Hammond.

"He loved the world, but his heart remained in Hammond," he said.

[reprinted by permission of the Times]

Folks waiting in line to pay their respects at the funeral.

Appendix 2

HE FOLLOWING IS THE text of the news releases given by the Hyles family beginning on January 31, 2001. These memos, which could be accessed on the Internet at the "baptist-city.com" site, from the Hyles family kept the church family constantly updated regarding the status of Brother Hyles' health. We gratefully thank Brother and Mrs. Ken Christensen for their help in operating this website.

WEDNESDAY, JANUARY 31, 2001

At 3:30 P.M. Tuesday afternoon, Bro. Hyles was admitted to the hospital. Dr. Dennis Streeter, the attending physician, diagnosed Bro. Hyles as having suffered a heart attack. He is presently in Intensive Care in stable condition.

The next 24–48 hours are important.

The hospital and family are insisting that there be no phone calls, flowers, gifts or visits of any kind.

We will keep you informed, and we thank you for your thoughts and prayers.

Appendixes

THURSDAY, FEBRUARY 1, 2001, 4:35 P.M.

At 2:00 P.M. today, doctors performed an angiogram on Bro. Hyles. The procedure revealed three arteries in the heart were clogged 80–90 percent with two others that are clogged to a lesser degree. In addition, the aortic valve is 60 percent blocked.

Doctors are advising that he be airlifted to the University of Chicago Hospital for surgery to replace four to five arteries and to replace the aortic valve. The surgery carries a 15–20 percent risk factor. There is also the presence of a lung infection that is causing a fever. However, the doctors do not feel that the infection should hinder the surgery.

Surgery will be performed either this evening or tomorrow morning. A new update will be issued immediately following the surgery.

Just as a reminder, at the insistence of the family and the hospital, please, no cards, gifts, flowers, visits or phone calls will be accepted at the hospital.

Thank you for your prayers and concerns.

FRIDAY, FEBRUARY 2, 2001, 9:40 A.M.

Bro. Hyles was flown to the University of Chicago Hospital late last evening. He is stable but still classified in critical condition. He has a balloon pump in his chest to assist his heart.

The doctors feel it is best to wait until Monday for surgery until more fluid has been drained from his lungs. This will assist his heart in recovery from the surgery.

Preacher is alert and his mind is sharp. He does still have severe pains in his back. His family has confidence in the present doctors and staff and feel postponing the surgery is wise.

The Passing Over of Dr. Jack Hyles

Thank you for your prayers. Please continue to pray because Preacher is still in critical condition.

SATURDAY, FEBRUARY 3, 2001, 6:00 P.M.

Bro. Hyles' condition remains critical but stable. He will undergo surgery Monday morning around 8:00 A.M. at the University of Chicago Hospital. He will have four or five bypasses as well as a valve replacement.

The surgery is expected to last from six to eight hours. As soon as the surgeon meets with the family, an update will be posted on this web site.

Although Bro. Hyles is experiencing some severe pain, he is in very good spirits. The family is extremely optimistic but covets everyone's prayers. Bro. Hyles was very pleased when he learned that his surgeon is a born-again Christian. Bro. Hyles is dreading the surgery but is at peace concerning the need of it and is not afraid.

When asked if there was anything he needed, his one request was for a Diet Dr. Pepper. Bro. Hyles has kept his sense of humor and sarcasm, and has teased with the nurses and the staff, even in his pain.

Mrs. Hyles appreciates the many prayers of everyone as well as honoring their privacy during this time.

MONDAY, FEBRUARY 5, 2001, 1:30 P.M.

Bro. Hyles was taken into surgery around 9:00 A.M. this morning. At 1:00 P.M. the family got a report from the surgeon that they are halfway through the surgery and everything is going

Appendixes

well. The entire surgery will take six to eight hours, and an update will be posted as soon as a report is received from the doctors.

Thank you for your prayers and concern. Your love is felt and appreciated by all here in Hammond.

MONDAY, FEBRUARY 5, 2001, 4:35 P.M.

The doctors have reported to the family that they are finished with the bypass part of the operation. In the process of doing the bypasses, they found that one other valve needs to be replaced.

They are entering into the valve replacement part of the surgery, which is the most critical part, and it is expected to take another two hours. The doctors say that Bro. Hyles is holding up well.

We are hoping for an update from the doctors around 6:00 P.M. central time. Thank you again for all of your prayers on behalf of the Hyles family.

MONDAY, FEBRUARY 5, 2001, 5:45 P.M.

Bro. Hyles is out of surgery at this time. He did have a second heart attack just prior to going into surgery which caused the doctors to go into emergency heart surgery procedures. During the surgery, four arteries were bypassed and two valves were replaced.

He is currently in extremely critical condition and will remain in the operating room for one and one-half hours. He will remain in extremely critical condition for the entire night.

The Passing Over of Dr. Jack Hyles

Your prayers are critical to his recovery and deeply appreciated by the family.

We will have another update in the morning. Thank you for your prayers.

MONDAY, FEBRUARY 5, 2001, 9:00 P.M.

Dr. Hyles is in extremely critical condition. The next 24 hours to seven days are critical. Doctors are keeping Dr. Hyles heavily medicated until late tomorrow afternoon; if he stabilizes they will begin to revive him.

Doctors performed quadruple bypass and replaced two heart valves. When Dr. Hyles was brought into the operating room he had a second heart attack, which would have been fatal if it had occurred outside of the operating room.

While in surgery, Dr. Hyles had an aneurysm of the heart wall and excessive bleeding. Surgery lasted over eight hours. The surgeon is guardedly optimistic.

These are critical hours for Dr. Hyles. The Hyles family covets your prayers at this time.

Tomorrow afternoon a special message will be given from the Hyles family regarding the surgery and the related circumstances.

TUESDAY, FEBRUARY 6, 2001, 12:00 P.M.

This is an official statement from the Hyles family. This morning at 9:43 A.M., Dr. Jack Hyles went to be with the Lord. His family was at his side in his final hours. He was free of pain at the time of his death.

Appendixes

The family is grateful for the prayers of people all over the world. Funeral arrangements are incomplete at this time, but will be announced as soon as possible.

The family request that no flowers or food be sent to the Hyles' home, but they do covet your continued prayers. Although we lost a husband, father, grandfather, and brother, we are aware that this is not our loss alone, but that millions all over the world share with us in our sense of great grief.

Bro. Hyles touched millions of lives, even those who attended him in those final hours.

Appendix 3

Jack Frasure Hyles

He Will Be Remembered

A remarkable man is gone now,
and this world seems
a little lessened somehow
because he is not a part of it...
a little less wise and great,
a little less good and brave.
But it helps to know that he
will never be forgotten
by those whose lives he touched.
And may our cherished memories
bring us comfort.

We all share in the tremendous loss of a pastor, mentor, friend, and servant. We, the Hyles family, would like to thank all of you for your acts of kindness, the many thousands of cards and letters of affection, the beautiful flowers and plants, and the many thoughts and much coveted prayers during this difficult season.

Appendixes

We who have lost a husband, brother, father, father-in-law, and grandfather understand the universal loss to all who loved our pastor. The truths that his life embodied will carry on through those on whom he has had the most profound influence: his congregation and friends. His life was a balanced blend of strength and beauty mingled with grace and truth with a dash of blue denim and lace. D. L. Moody once said, "the world has yet to see what God can do with a man totally surrendered to Him." We think that man lived among us in the life of Dr. Jack Hyles, and he will be greatly missed.

The Hyles family

One of the sweetest and the most overwhelming things was the multitudes of floral arrangements that were delivered to the church. The church looked like a garden. I decided in this book that we would do what Dad would do; we would say thank you to all of those who sent flowers. Following is as accurate of a list as we could compile from the florist cards we received after the funeral and memorial service. Please have mercy on us as we relied on others to help us at this time.

Pastor John Heath and Calvary Baptist Church, Keokuk, Iowa
Dr. Marc Rhodes and First Baptist Church of South Brevard, Florida
Pastor Mike Lovell and Lighthouse Baptist Temple
First Baptist Church of Rosemount, Minnesota
Faith Baptist Church, Berne, Indiana
Pastor Carillo and Lighthouse Baptist Church
Dr. and Mrs. Ken Graham and Victory Baptist Church, Benton, Arkansas
Montecito Park Baptist Church, Los Angeles, California

The Passing Over of Dr. Jack Hyles

Pastor Terry Anglea and Faith Baptist Church, Bourbonnais, Illinois

Highland Park Baptist Church & Tennessee Temple Schools, Chattanooga, Tennessee

Pastor Ralph Wingate and Calvary Baptist Church, Normal, Illinois

Pastor Eric Capaci and Gospel Light Baptist Church, Hot Springs, Arkansas

Calvary Bible Baptist Church, Willingboro, New Jersey

Longview Baptist Temple & Texas Baptist College, Dr. Bob Gray and Family, Longview, Texas

Grace Baptist Church

Hillside Baptist Church, Hixson, Tennessee

Pastor Terry Minge and Bethel Baptist Church, Spanaway, Washington

Pastor Barry Lee and First Baptist Church of Sauk Village, Illinois

Victory Baptist Church, West Portsmouth, Ohio

Danny and Cherie Brannon and Sharon Baptist Church, Swanee, Georgia

Dr. Rick Fox and First Baptist Church of Kenmore, Ohio

Pastor Ron Bankson and Gospel Light Baptist Church, Salisbury, North Carolina

First Baptist Church, Mediapolis, Iowa

Pastor Steven Byrd and Berean Baptist Church, Fayetteville, North Carolina

Pastor Zane Abberger and Lakeview Baptist Church, Lakeview, Michigan

Pastor Sisson and Bethel Baptist Church of Alta, Missouri

Dr. Clyde Box and Pastor Russell Jones, Brookhaven Baptist Church

Dr. Ken Pledger and the Calvary Baptist Church family

Pastor Thomas L. King and the New Testament Baptist Church, Hanford, California

Pastor C. F. Dowdey and Crestwood Baptist Church, Tyrone, Georgia

Lava Avenue Baptist Church, Wheeling, West Virginia

Brother and Mrs. Bob Wills, Mountain Park Baptist Church

Pastor Randall Hisaw and family, Greater Meridian Baptist Church

Pastor and Mrs. Gary Dice and Grace Baptist Church, Pittsfield, Illinois

Dr. and Mrs. Jim Vineyard and Windsor Hills Baptist Church, Oklahoma

Appendixes

Metropolitan Baptist Church

Dr. Richard Wallace and Temple Baptist Church, Lewisville, Texas

Dr. Bill Wininger and King's Way Baptist Church, Douglasville, Georgia

Pastor Robert Ross and Heritage Baptist Church, Jeannette, Pennsylvania

Hyles Baptist Church, Richmond, Virginia

Guin Baptist Church, Guin, Alabama

First Baptist Church of Morley, Michigan

Pastor Dean Miller and Cornerstone Baptist Church, Colorado Springs, Colorado

Pastor Kelly Howard and Newton County Baptist Church, Kentland, Indiana

Dr. Tom Neal and Berean Baptist Church, Orange Park, Florida

Ridgewood Baptist Church, Joilet, Illinois

Dr. D. Juaken Dumas, Mt. Pisgah Baptist Church

Victory Hill Baptist Church, Dallas, North Carolina

Pastor Jon Jenkins and the Grace Baptist Church family, Gaylord, Michigan

Pastor and Mrs. Rice of Peoples Baptist Church, Owensboro, Kentucky

Dr. Ron Baity and Berean Baptist Church, North Carolina

Dr. Stoddard and the New Testament Baptist Church, East Hartford, Connecticut

Pastor Walt Stowe and Calvary Baptist Church, Roy, Washington

Pastor and Members of Emmanuel Baptist Church

Pastor and Mrs Don Kiper, Bible Baptist Church, Niagara Falls, Ontario, Canada

Dr. Mike Mutchler and Grand View Baptist Church, Beavercreek, Oregon

Dr. Gary Herring and Bible Baptist Church, Uniontown, Pennsylvania

Pastor Max Hudson and Shadow Mountain Baptist, Morgan Hill, California

Pastor Dale Hart and Community Brethren Baptist Church, Pierceton, Indiana

Pastor Clyde Eborn and Grace Baptist Church, North Carolina

The Passing Over of Dr. Jack Hyles

Pastor Scott Christiansen and Frankfort Baptist Temple, Frankfort, Indiana

Pastor Jerry Wilson and Heritage Baptist Church, E. Palmyra, New York

Pastor and Mrs. John Shook, Bailey's Grove Baptist Church, Asheboro, North Carolina

Lakeside Baptist Church, Cedar Lake, Indiana

Johnny Pope and Christ Church Baptist Fellowship

Mt. Salem Baptist Church, West Union, West Virginia

Pastor Lane Briggs and the Greater Fall River Church, Fall River, Massachusetts

Clint and Candy Miller and North County Baptist Church, Escondido, California

Dr. Rock Vearfield and Forrest Hills Baptist Church, Decatur, Georgia

Pastor R. K. Young and Indian Hills Baptist Church, Shreveport, Louisiana

Gospel Light Baptist Church, Refton, Pennsylvania

Dr. John Hanks and Friends of Sauk Village Baptist Church, Sauk Village, Illinois

Faith Baptist Church, Belle Plaine, Iowa

Pastor Lenny Coates, Old-Fashioned Baptist Church, Yeagertown, Pennsylvania

Dr. Gary Coleman and Lavon Drive Baptist Church, Garland, Texas

Pastor Tony Hutson and Middle Tennessee Baptist Church, Murfreesboro, Tennessee

Pomerado Road Baptist Church, Poway, California

Faith Baptist Church of Colorado Springs, Colorado

Westside Baptist Church of Laurinburg, North Carolina

Pastor and Mrs. Jim Beller and the Arnold Baptist Tabernacle Church Family

Heritage Baptist Church of Wallingford, Connecticut

Pastor Rick Finley and Fellowship Baptist Church, Durham, North Carolina

Mike Creed and Independent Baptist Church, Clinton, Maryland

Dr. Joe W. Myers, Kerwin Baptist Church, Kernersville, North Carolina

Appendixes

Pastor and Mrs. Mickey Carter, Landmark Baptist Church, Haines City, Florida

Antioch Baptist Church of Warren, Michigan

Prairie Creek Bible Baptist Church, Mesquite, Texas

Pastor Hampton and Barstow Baptist Temple

Pastor J. Callaway, Hammond First Assembly of God Church family

Pastor Carrillo and Lighthouse Baptist Church

Pastor Marvin Dennis, Carson City, Nevada

Dr. Harry Boyle of Grace Baptist Church, Portland, Maine

W.D.S., Bethel Baptist Church of Sligo, Pennsylvania

Pastor Foust and members of Pinelevel Baptist Church

Pastor and Mrs. Jim Baize, Midway Baptist Church, San Diego, California

Pastor James Seaman and Victory Baptist Church of Peotone, Illinois

Pastor David R. Cox and Seattle Baptist Church, Seattle, Washington

Dr. Les Hobbins and Lewis Avenue Baptist Church, Temperance, Michigan

Pastor and Mrs. Dave Carlson and Gospel Baptist Church, Manchester, New Hampshire

Pastor Dean Noonan and Faith Baptist Church, Milwaukee, Wisconsin

Community Baptist Church, Millington, Michigan

Dr. and Mrs. Michael Haynes and Trident Baptist Church, N. Charleston, South Carolina

Pastor Dave Baker and Lighthouse Baptist Church, Columbia, Tennessee

Pastor John Barnes and Hines Chapel Baptist Church, Greensboro, North Carolina

Dr. John Vaprezsan and Metro Baptist Church, Belleville, Michigan

Emmanuel Baptist Church, Morgantown, West Virginia

Lighthouse Baptist Church, Miamisburg, Ohio

Pastor Silva and Fundamental Baptist Church

Pastor John Paisley and Riverview Baptist Church, Pasco, Washington

Roloff Evangelistic Enterprises, Corpus Christi, Texas

Pastor Costantino and Lighthouse Baptist Church, N. Tonawanda, New York

The Passing Over of Dr. Jack Hyles

Wylewood Baptist Church, Oshkosh, Wisconsin

Rosedale Baptist Church, Baltimore, Maryland

Pastor and Mrs. John Doss and Bible Baptist Church, Greenfield, Ohio

Pastor and Mrs. Cruse and Shining Light Baptist Church

Pastor Walters and Southside Baptist Church of Rock Hill, South Carolina

Dr. Aiken and Tabernacle Baptist Church and Ministries, Greenville, South Carolina

Pastor Todd Poynter and Greenwood Bible Baptist Church, Greenwood, Indiana

Pastor Mark Smith and Faith Baptist Church, Tacoma, Washington

Newtown Baptist Church

Canyon Creek Baptist Church, Richardson, Texas

Dr. Bobby Roberson and Gospel Light Baptist Church, Walkertown, North Carolina

David Wood Ministry and David Wood Ministry Staff

Dr. Mike Cox and F.B.M.I. Staff, Schererville, Indiana

Revival Fires and the Dennis Corle family

Dr. Elmer Fernandez and *Fires of Evangelism*

Pastor and Mrs. Mark Monte and Faith Baptist Church, Avon, Indiana

Three Rivers Baptist Church, Fort Wayne, Indiana

Pastor and Mrs. Walt McDaniel and Bow Baptist Church, Vermont

Pastor Jack Cox and Liberty Baptist Church, Durham, North Carolina

Pastor and Mrs. Robert Ueltzen and First Baptist Church, Crete, Illinois

Pastor and Mrs. Sheldon Schearer and Heritage Baptist Church, Great Falls, Montana

Pastor Dave Solt and Parkview Baptist Church, London, England

Dr. and Mrs. Gary Berry and Liberty Baptist Church Family, Charlotte, North Carolina

Dr. Chris Brown and East Coast Baptist Church, Virginia Beach, Virginia

Cornerstone Baptist Church, Chapel Hill, North Carolina; The Bill Davis Family

The Friendship Baptist Youth Group, Cincinnati, Ohio

Appendixes

Pastor Proctor and Westwood Baptist Church, Poplar Bluff, Missouri

Emmanuel Baptist Church and Midwestern Baptist College, Pontiac, Michigan

Bible Baptist Church, Griffith, Indiana

Pastor Marty Braemer and Ford's Bush Baptist Church, Fort Plaine, New York

Pastor and Mrs. Bob Heath and Maplewood Bible Baptist Church, Chicago, Illinois

Pastor Doug Anderson and Bible Baptist Church, Newman, Georgia

Dr. Ralph Sexton and Trinity Baptist Church, Asheville, North Carolina

Friends of Emmanuel Baptist Church

Pastor Tim Booth and Haughton Baptist Temple, Haughton, Louisiana

Metropolitan Baptist Church

Bible Baptist Church, Pastor Durgin and Church Family

Pastor Bob Baines and Eastside Baptist Church, Everett, Washington

Temple Baptist Church of Kokomo, Indiana

Dr. Jeff Fugate and Clays Mill Road Baptist Church, Lexington, Kentucky

Gospel Light Baptist Church, Evington, Virginia

Bull Run Baptist Church, Manassas, Virginia

Heartland Baptist Church

Pembina Valley Baptist Church, Winkler, Manitoba, Canada

Mike and Brenda Sullivant

Pastor Wayne Walters and First Baptist Church of Cahokia, Illinois

Koolau Baptist Church

Dr. Richard Skiver and Bethel Baptist Church, Ravenna, Ohio

Pastor Waybright and Victory Baptist Church, Hermiston, Oregon

Pastor and Mrs. Andy Edwards III and Northwest Baptist Church of Toledo, Ohio

Dave and Dawn Morrissey and Parkview Baptist Church, North Lake, Illinois

Pastor and Mrs. Dann Patrick and Dr. and Mrs. Richard Cordell, FWBC, Goldsboro, North Carolina

Pastor and Mrs. James Caskey and Faith Baptist Church, Barberton, Ohio

The Passing Over of Dr. Jack Hyles

Calvary Baptist Church, Culpeper, Virginia

Faith Baptist Church, Richmond, Kentucky

Pastor William Duttry and First Baptist Church of Ohio

Grace Baptist Church, Beaver Dams, New York

Lighthouse Baptist Church, Cortez, Colorado; Larry Chappell

Sugar Creek Baptist Church

Baptist International Missions, Inc.; Dr. and Mrs Don Sisk; Dr. and Mrs Roy Thompson; and World Missions Center Staff, Chattanooga, Tennessee

Pastor Carl Stevens and Greater Grace World Outreach

Dr. Don Smith and Shenandoah Bible Baptist Church, Martinsburg, West Virginia

Pastor Bobby Toler and North Sharon Baptist Church, Grass Lake, Michigan

The Christian Jew Foundation, San Antonio, Texas; Gary Hedrick and staff

Dr. Paul Chappell and Lancaster Baptist Church and West Coast Baptist College, Lancaster, California

Pastor and Mrs. Stanley and Valley Independent Baptist Church, Huttonsville, West Virginia

Pastor Bill McSpadden and Pleasantville Baptist Church, Pleasantville, Iowa

Pastor Thomas Crank and Madeira Baptist Church, Cincinnati, Ohio

Pastor Dan Parton and Timberline Baptist Church, Manitou Springs, Colorado

Pastor Mark Turner and Foothill Baptist Church, Moreno Valley, California

Pastor Lonnie Mattingly and Shawnee Baptist Church, Louisville, Kentucky

Dr. and Mrs. Mike Monte and Calvary Baptist Church, Robbinsdale, Minnesota

Dr. and Mrs. Bob Gray, Missionaries to Germany

Pastor and Mrs. Corey Bane and Grace Baptist Church, Delaware, Ohio

Pastor Messer and Trinity Baptist Church, Jacksonville, Florida

Appendixes

Dr. and Mrs. Darrell Cox and Trinity Baptist Church, Mocksville, North Carolina

Pastor Lyle Dye and Battlecreek Baptist Temple

Joyful Woman Magazine; Roger and Joy Rice Martin

Dr. Jack Trieber and North Valley Baptist Church, Santa Clara, California

Sword of the Lord; Dr. Shelton Smith, Murfreesboro, Tennessee

Hopewell Baptist Church, Napa, California

Pastor and Mrs. Keith Wall and First Baptist Church of Iron Mountain, Michigan

Pastor Wayne Musatics and Central Baptist Church and school, Granite City, Illinois

Pastor Charles Copeland and Emmanuel Baptist Church, Lemont, Delaware

Ebeye Baptist Church, Republic of Marshall Island

Pastor and Mrs. Francis Grillone and Independent Baptist Church, Bellans Falls, Vermont

Dr. Ray Hancock and Southwide Baptist Fellowship

Pilgrim Baptist Church, Gastonia, North Carolina; the Anderson Family

Pastor and Mrs. Gerald Collingsworth and Heritage Baptist Church, Mogadore, Ohio

First Baptist Church, Elkton, South Dakota

Pastor D. Hill and Nepean Baptist Church, Urch Penrith, Australia

The Paul Vineyard family, Missionaries to the Philippines

Dr. Tom and Joyce Malone, Pontiac, Michigan

The Curtis Hutson Family

The John R. Rice Family

Dr. and Mrs. Randy Taylor and Family

Dr. and Mrs. Don Boyd and Luke

Dr. and Mrs. Carl Hatch

Dr. and Mrs. Lee Roberson

Verle and Lucille Ackerman

Dr. Joe Boyd

Dr. Dennis Streeter and Family

The Passing Over of Dr. Jack Hyles

Pastor and Charlene Johnston
Dr. and Mrs. Larry May
Pastor Tom Lemmons and Family, Missoula, Montana
Dr. and Mrs. James A. Jones and Jason
Pastor and Mrs. Mark Maddox and Family, Guin, Alabama
Pastor Bob McIntosh
Dr. and Mrs. Ray Warren and Family
Rev. Mike Bragg
Faculty and Staff of Northern Baptist Bible College of Dunbar, Wisconsin
Heartland Baptist Bible College, Sam Davison and Jeff Copes
Golden State Baptist College, Santa Clara, California
Pensacola Christian College Administration and Faculty and Dr. and Mrs. Donald Horton, Pensacola, Florida
The Maranatha College Family, Watertown, Wisconsin
Baptist Bible College Faculty and Staff
Badger State Baptist School, 5th and 6th Grade, Milwaukee, Wisconsin
Dr. and Mrs. Andy Koultouridis
Bruce, Carol, Joshua and Jason Webb
Mr. and Mrs. Giragos and Family
David, Linda, Melissa, and Bethany Stubblefield
The Steve Pritchards
The Dan Cavenders
Zana Reichen
The Wolfes
The Ken Osborn Family
Russell and Maxine Anderson
Roger and Carolyn Dock and Family
Richard and Pamela Wilkins
Fred and Mary Singleton
Wendell and Marlene Evans
Neil and Kathy Fruit and sons
The Jeff Ryder Family
The Robert Auclair Family

Appendixes

Tom, Jane, and Carissa Grafton
Larry and Estelle Smith and Family
The Glen Morris Family
Dr. and Mrs. Jeff Owens and Family
Thom, Cathy, Annie and T.J. Kimmel
Jeff, Craig, Karen, Linda, Sue, Randy, and Susanne
Keith Wyrick Family
David, Amy, and Timothy Sisson
Wayne and Martha Matheson
Ray, Gail, Stephanie, April, John and Heather Allen
Mike and Cindy Schaap and Family
Govea Family
The Danny Coffey Family
Rob and Deb Ward
The Cal Streeter Family
David Reynolds and Trina Staton
Paul and Jolie Sock, Missionaries to Poland
Ed and Michelle McCarter
John and Sharon Marples
Jerry and Doris Smith
Tim and Betty McCurdy and Mrs. Wilma Robinson
Jerry and Susan Pitsilides
Mary Pitsilides
J. B. and Betty Buffington
David and Angela Carpenter and children, Pleasantville, Iowa
The Durhams
The Rick Nelson Family
The Ken Frizzell Family
Becky and Mitchell Burkhart
The Dolan Family
The Jack DeCoster Family
Tony, Maria, Anthony, David, Daniel, Cassandra and Alex Rivera
Lee, Teresa, Joshua, Jordan, Jared, Nicholas, Nathan and Jack Comstock
Paul, Judy and Matthew Melton

The Passing Over of Dr. Jack Hyles

Tom and Heather Knoezer
Kevin and Loretta Walker and Family
Bob and JoBeth Hooker and Daughters
Carlos and Sarah Rivera
Robert and Rose Pearson
Harvey and Dianne Robinson
Gary and Susan Harper
Gary and Ada Harper
Tammy Harper
James and Sarah Blalock Family
The John Swift Family
Susan Matchie and Ron Swift
Brother Victor Hernandez
Mr. and Mrs. Peter Solan Jr. and Family
Dick and Joanne Ross and Family
Wayne and Robin Webb Family
Kirk and Betty Beard
Kirk and April Beard
Jeff and Beth Rardin
George and Mary Vogel
The Ed Mattingly Family
Pastor and Carolyn Riggs
Sharlight Family
Bessie Reyher and Family
Rick, Becky, Ricky, and Rachel Martin, Missionaries to the Philippines
Rick, Iva, Heather, Heidi, and Holly Bartley
Tom, Genevieve, and Rachel Atchison
Beth Woodard and Mark Smitherman
Mark and Christina Tossell
Brother and Mrs. Richard Tudor
Billy Colsten, Louise Blakely, Roger and Alice Salewsky and Kim
    Salewsky

Steve, Laura, Tracie, Michael, Jennifer, and Cheryl Larsen

Appendixes

Paul, Rhonda, Alana, Samuel and Miguel Fierro
The Cosaloom Family
The Mathewson Family
The DiCicco Family of New Jersey
Lorna Lydick and Ester Bloom
Michael and Amy Ray and Family
The Tim Harrells
Garrett and Patty Moseley
David and Tina Douglass and Family
John and Cynthia Francis and Children
The Lee Family
Kyle and Shirley Johnson
Jeff, Stephanie, Lauren, and Micah Johnson
Steve, Tara, Mikayla and Kaleb Kirby
Gina and Chris Miller
Joe and Judi Freeman
Charlie and Barb Freyermuth
Terry and Ann Duff
Mark and Priscilla Duff
Charlie and Mindy Rousey
Tom and Girlis Bennett
Darwin and Chris and Children
Chris Elrod and Marge DelosReyes
Ricardo Valdez, Jr.
Matias and Johnathan Valdez
The Highfills
Dwayne, Anna, Candice, Aaron and Krystle Wilson
The Scheck Family
The Dowdey Family
Duane and Judy Jacobs and Family
Becky, Adam, and Amber Bryan
Chester Mulligan
Ray and Debi Young and Family
Bill and Patsy Burr

The Passing Over of Dr. Jack Hyles

David, Sharon, Alice, Melinda and Bonnie
Boyd and Sheryl Woodward
Evangelist Monte and Jan Watts
Frank, Linda, Lynn, Kip and Karen Porter
The Bill Grady Family, Knoxville, Tennessee
Brother David Michaels and Family, Glen Gary, West Virginia
Helen, Denise, Blandi, Ron, Buddy Jr. and Ilene
Tom McDermott
Johnny, Susan, Amanda, Wesley, and Renee Day
Dave, Michele, Heather and David Gilbert
The Rynberks
The Jimmy Rogers Family; Ann — Former Grade School Faculty
Mickey – H.B.H.S. Class of 1978
David – H.B.H.S. Class of 1979
Jenny Lynn Rogers Rodman
The Greg Pyne Family
Michael and Helen Britton
Mrs. Shirley Comer
Jim, Suzanne, Mark, and Sharon Maxwell
The Lail Family
Albert Payton
Ray and Mabel Boardway
Pete and Julie Richter
Mike and Debbie Borsh
Dan and Kathleen Sigstad
David and Penny Parshall
Arlys Cooper
Richard and Pam White
Chris and Dawn Moncado and Family
Lisa Stoddard and Father
Johnny and Ana Molina
Karla, Enrique, and Marta
Monica Nagore and Family
Tom and Erma McKinney

Appendixes

Keith, Lynn, Justin, and Heather McKinney
Phil, Gail, Adam and Abbey Merhalski
Dale and Joan Vernander
Martin, Sheri, Rebecca and Rachel Laing
The Mike Botte Family
Phil and Tabatha Edge
Judge and Mrs. James Clement
Mayor Duane, Lori, Alex and Maggie Dedelow
White Insurance; Mr. and Mrs. Tom White and Mr. and Mrs. Ted
      Havens
Your Family from Garland Police Department Staff
Service Division; Bank One
Yingling Family and All Your Friends at Yingling Cleaners
Gary Murphy and All at Ray's Roofing
Congress Enterprises and Staff
City Sales, Inc.
UGN of Chicago Heights, Illinois
UGN of Valparaiso, Indiana
UGNC; Shift Employees
Americal Corporation
Alpha Beta Press
Overnite Transportation Company, South Holland, Illinois Terminal
TruGreen-ChemLawn, Crestwood, Illinois
Temperature Engineering
Greater Hammond Community Services
United Parcel Services; John Hampton and Jerry Phillips
Midwest Fastener
Calumet Travel
Illinois School Bus Company
Your Friends at Domain Communications
Tyson Lincoln Mercury; Linda Pote
The Hyles-Anderson College Students, Faculty, and Staff
Baptist Boys Battalion Boys Club
Hyles-Anderson College Clinic Staff

The Passing Over of Dr. Jack Hyles

The Spanish Department, First Baptist Church of Hammond, Indiana
Sailor Ministry, First Baptist Church of Hammond, Indiana
Fred and Heather Singleton and the H.A.C. Americal Girls
Young-at-Heart Couples Class, First Baptist Church of Hammond
The Pathfinders Department, First Baptist Church of Hammond
Far Above Rubies Club
Sophomore Class of 2003, Hammond Baptist High School
First Baptist Church Staff
Hammond Baptist Schools Business Office
Blue Denim and Lace Girls Club
Oriental Ministry, First Baptist Church of Hammond, Indiana
First Baptist Church Teenagers
City Baptist Middle School Faculty, Staff, and Students
The Junior Class of Hammond Baptist High School
Board of Deacons, First Baptist Church of Hammond
The B-7 Bus Route and the Watchmen Bible Club; Derek and Bridget
    Morgan
Junior I Department, First Baptist Church of Hammond, Indiana
Ladies of the Philippines Circle; Women's Missionary Society
Hammond Baptist High School, Class of 2000
First Baptist Church Custodians
Brother Darrell Moore's Staff, Hyles-Anderson College
Adult Church Choir, First Baptist Church of Hammond, Indiana
Sweetheart Couples Class, First Baptist Church of Hammond, Indiana
The Bible Club Bus Ministry, First Baptist Church of Hammond, Indiana
Brother Johnny Colsten and The New Life Class, First Baptist Church of
    Hammond, Indiana
Dr. Jack Schaap's Staff at Hyles-Anderson College
Brother John Francis and Division One, First Baptist Church of
    Hammond, Indiana
Christian Womanhood
Brother Roy Moffitt and the Friendly Couples Class, First Baptist Church
    of Hammond, Indiana
Hammond Baptist High School

Appendixes

Hammond Baptist High School, Class of 1999

The Junior High I-A Sunday School Department, First Baptist Church of Hammond, Indiana

High School Department, Elaine and Crew, First Baptist Church of Hammond, Indiana

Hammond Baptist Junior High School

"A" Bus #16 and the Sylaidis Family, First Baptist Church of Hammond, Indiana

Bus 72-C Workers, Wendell Cox, the Billingsleys, and the Snow families, First Baptist Church of Hammond, Indiana

Junior High II Department Teachers, First Baptist Church of Hammond, Indiana

Deaf Department, First Baptist Church of Hammond, Indiana

B-1 Bus Route, Brother and Mrs. Rick Sparks, First Baptist Church of Hammond, Indiana

Kelly Cervantes and the Mexico Circle, W.M.S., First Baptist Church of Hammond, Indiana

Security Department, Hyles-Anderson College

Division 8, First Baptist Church of Hammond, Indiana

City Baptist Junior Class and Mrs. R. M. Jackson

The Hammond Baptist High School, Class of 1996

"A" Bus 32, First Baptist Church of Hammond, Indiana

Hammond Baptist High School, Class of 2001

Hammond Baptist High School Bus Route

Appendix 4

My Preacher, Dr. Jack Hyles
by Dennis Streeter, M.D.

FIRST MET MY GOOD friend and my preacher, Dr. Jack Hyles, when I moved to the Chicago area to attend medical school. We had a tremendous relationship, and he was a man's man, a preacher's preacher, and a true friend. Many times we talked in the study, and I was tickled to death to realize that the preacher was concerned about me, my work, and what happened in my life. Preacher was just fantastic to always be the friend who remembered the little things and put a person at ease.

During all of this time, Preacher had a few medical concerns, but nothing of tremendous significance. Between 1975 and 1976, Preacher was diagnosed with a hiatal hernia. He and I discussed this situation many times and decided not to perform any surgical procedure on it. Preacher continued to be in reasonably good health, though he had some hypertension. Preacher would always say to me, "Dennis, don't tell me how my heart's doing and how my blood pressure is. Don't really want to know."

Many times as we saw each other during the ensuing several

Appendixes

years, we would talk, and I would say, "Preacher, let's check your heart and your blood pressure."

He would say, "No, no. I don't want to do that. I don't want anyone to know what's going on with my heart. My heart is fine; it's doing good."

As time went on, during the 1990s, Preacher would say, "I've got this back pain. My back pain is quite significant."

He had pneumonia on one occasion, and he still had the back pain. He would still say, "Dennis, I don't want to know anything about my heart, and please don't check over my heart."

During these episodes, and during these times of visiting with the preacher and talking to him, he would say, "My heart's doing fine. I'm doing great." He always had to run here and there, keeping up with his busy schedule.

Preacher would always relate that his heart was doing fine, and he was feeling good; but he always mentioned that he had back pain over the last several years. I discussed his echocardiogram that he had done at Mayo Clinic in 1999 with him. The test showed that his heart had a reasonable contraction but was not as good as a normal heart. He still felt he was doing fine.

Then in the last 12 days before he passed away, he called me and he called Mrs. Kris Grafton, the head nurse at Hyles-Anderson College, and said that he was having some difficulty with breathing and that he had also had some problems while in Mexico. When I spoke with Preacher, I asked him to meet me at the Broadway Methodist Hospital Emergency Room on January 27, a Saturday.

Preacher came to the Emergency Room, and said he had severe back pain. He mentioned that he felt really uncomfortable

The Passing Over of Dr. Jack Hyles

lying down and could not lie down to sleep. He said he had severe back pain while in Mexico.

We did a chest x-ray and blood work, and we found fluid in the lung area and around the lung. I felt that we needed to make sure that he did not have some problem with his aorta because ballooning on the aorta would cause severe back pain. At that point, we did a CAT scan which showed a continued problem with fluid around the lung, but he said, "Please don't ask me to have an electrocardiogram. I don't want to know anything about the heart."

I pushed the preacher a little bit, and he said, "Dennis, I don't want to know anything about my heart."

"Preacher, I think you have some congestive heart failure. At least that's what it appears to be," I said. "I know you have some arthritis in your back; we could see that on the CAT scan. You also have a little bit of rash on your back, probably due to the heating pad. Or maybe it has a viral type of cause." I was unsure about the rash. At that point, we wanted to go ahead and give him at least some water pills to take off some of the fluid—even though he was rather sensitive about having anything checked in his heart.

I called him on Sunday night. He was still having some shortness of breath and difficulty with lying down due to severe back pain. We had given him some pain medication to control this pain. On Monday night, I called back again, and we decided to go further. I said, "We must meet you in the Emergency Room, and let's check over everything at this time."

I met him in the Emergency Room at Broadway Methodist Hospital on Tuesday, January 30, and Preacher said, "I'm having more difficulty."

Appendixes

"Preacher, we need to check everything now," I said. "We've kind of avoided checking this, and we need to check everything."

"Okay, Dennis," Preacher said, "I'm having too many difficulties in breathing."

So we did a chest x-ray which showed more fluid around the lungs, more congestive heart failure, and at that point, an EKG showed that he had had a myocardial infarction. We did an echocardiogram which is a sound wave check of the heart showing that his ejection fraction was very low, in the 20 percentile range, and that he had significant damage to his heart.

He was placed in Intensive Care and during this time, Preacher would say, "If they start working on my heart, Dennis, I'm done. I'm sure that I will not continue to make it any further." He mentioned this fact over and over again; he did not want to have anyone to start working on his heart. However, he realized at this point that there was no other choice, and that this was the real cause of his problem.

He improved on Wednesday; he was breathing better. However, on Thursday in the afternoon, he became more short of breath and had more difficulty. His oxygenation level went lower, and we felt we had to then do a cardiac catheterization. The cardiologist, Dr. Nazzal Obaid, is a good friend, and he said, "Dennis, we need to go to the Cath Lab."

We went to the Cath Lab, and tests showed that there was severe damage to the heart with an ejection fraction in the low 20's. An intra-aortic balloon pump was placed during that time. At that time, I consulted with a good friend of Preacher's and mine, Dr. Henry Giragos, a cardiac surgeon, because the choice had been made to send Brother Hyles to the University of Chicago. He needed an aortic valve replacement as well as

The Passing Over of Dr. Jack Hyles

several bypass surgeries at the same time. His heart was in such a damaged state from the myocardial infarction which apparently had taken place when he was preaching in Mexico the week prior to his coming to see us. The myocardial infarction was the primary cause of his problem. We felt that he should be transferred to the University of Chicago where they were doing valve surgery with acute cardiac situations as well as bypass surgeries.

Brother Hyles was transferred late Thursday night, early Friday morning, to the University of Chicago via helicopter with the balloon pump in place. During the time he spent at the University of Chicago Hospitals, many of the people said he was so friendly. The nurses would always say, "He was more concerned about us than himself." He continued to show concern for others during this time.

He was then taken to cardiac surgery on Monday, February 5, where the doctors found much more damage to the heart than they had realized. He had to have two valves replaced and several bypass surgeries. He continued to do poorly and eventually passed away on February 6, 2001.

Preacher was my friend. Preacher was my hero. He was a man's man, a preacher's preacher, a friend to everyone, and I considered him my friend. I loved him very much.

Appendix 5

HE FOLLOWING PEOPLE WERE such a blessing to the family as they performed various tasks for us. We thank you from the bottom of our hearts.

FUNERAL DIRECTORS:
Mr. John Ault, Bocken Funeral Home
Mrs. Linda Ault
Mr. Thom Kimmel

PALL BEARERS:
Jesse Browing, Craig Bush, Randy Ericson, Victor Hernandez, Bob Hooker, and Bill Schutt

HONORARY PALL BEARERS:
Bob Auclair, Don Boyd, Dave Douglass, Darrell Moore, Mike Sisson, and Tom Vogel

HONORARY PALL BEARERS:
Rick Bartley, Dale Breed, Lee Comstock, Mark Crockett, Phil Edge, Dave Sisson, Scott Tremaine, Clyde Wolfe, and Cliff Wroe

The Passing Over of Dr. Jack Hyles

HONOR GUARDS:

Steve Alberts, Louis Allen, Wilgus Allen, Mike Anderson, Bob Auclair, Tom Bensinger, Paul Benton, Donald Bohlayer, Mike Borsh, Don Boyd, Charlie Bulmer, Ray Chalifoux, Jon Condict, John Cooper, Keith Cowling, Chris Cox, Mike Cox, Mario Cuozzo, Dan Daniel, Leonard Delano, Tom Dewar, Allen Domelle, Mike Fish, John Francis, Neil Fruit, Jeff Gibson, Mike Goodall, Tom Grafton, Joe Hackett, Bill Hasse, Brian Hasse, Ray Highfill, Steve Huckins, Duane Jacobs, Doug Kalapp, David Long, John Mathewson, Jim Maxwell, Tom McConkey, Danny Mendez, Jim Meyer, Matt Millen, Stan Miller, Danny Mock, Elton Mock, Julio Molina, Rick Morgan, Bob Morris, Lee Mullins, Glen Munson, John Nocito, Jason Ogle, John Olsen, Jerry Ossewaarde, L. J. Parr, Jeff Peach, Bob Pearson, Mark Pfeifer, Norman Pfeiffer, Phil Pins, Jerry Pitsilides, Pete Richter, James Riley, Mike Rykhus, Phil Sallie, Michael Sarver, Andrew Scheltens, Owen Schipplein, Bill Schutt, Mike Sisson, Larry Smith, Ted Speer, Larry Staab, Ron Stapleton, Warren Storm, David Stubblefield, Gary Sumner, Chris Tefft, Don Tinsley, James VanderHoogt, Daryl Whitehouse, John Wilson, Wes Wilson, Joe Wittig, Dan Wolfe, Doug Wruck, and Tony Ye

SECURITY GUARDS:

Eddie Ayala, Rick Bartley, Chris Braye, Dale Breed, Aaron Bruski, Bruce Campbell, Joshua Comstock, Lee Comstock, Clyde Conner, Mark Crockett, Glenn Ealy, Phil Edge, Zachary Foust, Tim Harrell, Mark Hawthorne, Warren Heard, Terry Hedderman, Greg Jones, Doug Kollar, Giancarlo Leon, Paul Manwell, Ed Mattingly, Joseph Mercado, Dan Mohnkern, Oscar Moreno, Garrett Moseley, Bryan Nickel, Richard Nickel, Barry

Appendixes

Nixon, Andrew Ossewaarde, Mike Poch, Dave Sisson, Kevin Spink, Jake Suttles, Scott Tremaine, Greg Villaroman, Adam Wolfe, Clyde Wolfe, Pat Worland, and Cliff Wroe

HAMMOND POLICE OFFICERS:

Brian Abrams, Chris Berdine, John Crook, Mark Detterline, Gary Gleason, Tom Golfis, Don Kalina, Manny Llanes, Mark Malacinia, Shawn McDaniel, Phil Merritt, Tony Sonaty, Rich Tumidalsky, and Charles Turner

Appendix 6

REGISTRATION DISTRICT NO. **16.10**		STATE OF ILLINOIS		STATE FILE NUMBER
REGISTERED NUMBER		**MEDICAL CERTIFICATE OF DEATH**		**602039**

DECEASED–NAME	FIRST	MIDDLE	LAST		SEX	DATE OF DEATH (MONTH, DAY, YEAR)
1.	JACK	F.	HYLES		2 MALE	3 FEBRUARY 6, 2001

COUNTY OF DEATH		AGE–LAST BIRTHDAY (YRS)	UNDER 1 YEAR MOS / DAYS	UNDER 1 DAY HOURS / MIN	DATE OF BIRTH (MONTH, DAY, YEAR)
4. COOK		5a. 74	5b.	5c.	5d. SEPTEMBER 25, 1926

CITY, TOWN, TWP, OR ROAD DISTRICT NUMBER	HOSPITAL OR OTHER INSTITUTION - NAME (IF NOT IN EITHER, GIVE STREET AND NUMBER)	IF HOSP. OR INST. INDICATE D.O.A OR EMER. RM. INPATIENT (SPECIFY)
6a. CHICAGO	6b. THE UNIVERSITY OF CHICAGO HOSPITALS	6c INPATIENT

BIRTHPLACE (CITY AND STATE OR FOREIGN COUNTRY)	MARRIED, NEVER MARRIED, WIDOWED, DIVORCED (SPECIFY)	NAME OF SURVIVING SPOUSE (MAIDEN NAME IF WIFE)	WAS DECEASED EVER IN U.S. ARMED FORCES? (YES.NO)
7 Italy, TX.	8a. MARRIED	8b. Beverly J. Slaughter	9 Yes

SOCIAL SECURITY NUMBER	USUAL OCCUPATION	KIND OF BUSINESS OR INDUSTRY	EDUCATION (SPECIFY ONLY HIGHEST GRADE COMPLETED) Elementary Secondary (0-12)	College (1-4 or 5 +)
10. 450-30-0185	11a. Pastor	11b. Church	12	5+

RESIDENCE (STREET AND NUMBER)	CITY, TOWN, TWP, OR ROAD DISTRICT NO	INSIDE CITY (YES NO)	COUNTY
13a. 910 RIDGE ROAD / APT # 204	13b. Munster	13c. Yes	13d. Lake

STATE	ZIP CODE	RACE (WHITE, BLACK, AMERICAN INDIAN, etc.) (SPECIFY)	OF HISPANIC ORIGIN? (SPECIFY NO OR YES–IF YES SPECIFY CUBAN MEXICAN PUERTO RICAN etc.)
13e Indiana	13f. 46321	14a. White	14b XX NO ☐ YES SPECIFY:

FATHER–NAME	FIRST	MIDDLE	LAST	MOTHER–NAME	FIRST	MIDDLE	(MAIDEN) LAST
15.	Willis	Athey	Hyles	16.	Coystal	Mattie	Frasure

INFORMANT'S NAME (TYPE OR PRINT)	RELATIONSHIP	MAILING ADDRESS (STREET AND NO OR R F D, CITY OR TOWN, STATE, ZIP)
17a. MAYBLEINE GIGGERS	17b HOSPITAL RECORDS	17c. 5841 SOUTH MARYLAND CHICAGO, ILLINOIS 60637

18. PART I. Enter the diseases, or complications that caused the death. Do not enter the mode of dying, such as cardiac or respiratory arrest, shock, or heart failure. List only one cause on each line.

APPROXIMATE INTERVAL BETWEEN ONSET AND DEATH

Immediate Cause (Final disease or condition resulting in death)

(a) MYOCARDIAL INFARCTION
DUE TO, OR AS A CONSEQUENCE OF

CONDITIONS, IF ANY WHICH GIVE RISE TO IMMEDIATE CAUSE (a) STATING THE UNDERLYING CAUSE LAST.

(b) LEFT VENTRICULAR FAILURE
DUE TO, OR AS A CONSEQUENCE OF

(c)

PART II. Other significant conditions contributing to death but not resulting in the underlying cause given in PART I	AUTOPSY (YES NO)	WERE AUTOPSY FINDINGS AVAILABLE PRIOR TO COMPLETION OF CAUSE OF DEATH? (YES NO)
	19a. NO	19b.

DATE OF OPERATION, IF ANY	MAJOR FINDINGS OF OPERATION	IF FEMALE WAS THERE A PREGNANCY IN PAST THREE MONTHS?
20a.	20b.	20c. YES ☐ NO ☐

I (DID) (DID NOT) ATTEND THE DECEASED AND LAST SAW HIM/HER ALIVE ON (MONTH, DAY, YEAR)	WAS CORONER OR MEDICAL EXAMINER NOTIFIED? (YES.NO)	HOUR OF DEATH
21a. FEBRUARY 6, 2001	21b. YES	21c. 9:43 A.M.

TO THE BEST OF MY KNOWLEDGE, DEATH OCCURRED AT THE TIME, DATE AND PLACE AND DUE TO THE CAUSE(S) STATED		DATE SIGNED (MONTH, DAY, YEAR)
22a. SIGNATURE ▶		22b. FEBRUARY 6, 2001

NAME AND ADDRESS OF CERTIFIER (TYPE OR PRINT)		ILLINOIS LICENSE NUMBER
22c. DAVID WOO, MD	5841 SOUTH MARYLAND CHICAGO, ILLINOIS 60637	22d. 125-039882

NAME OF ATTENDING PHYSICIAN IF OTHER THAN CERTIFIER (TYPE OR PRINT)	NOTE: IF AN INJURY WAS INVOLVED IN THIS DEATH THE CORONER OR MEDICAL EXAMINER MUST BE NOTIFIED
23. DAVID V. JAYAKAR, MD	

BURIAL, CREMATION, REMOVAL (SPECIFY)	CEMETERY OR CREMATORY–NAME	LOCATION CITY OR TOWN / STATE	DATE (MONTH, DAY, YEAR)
24a. Entombment	24b. Memory Lane Memorial Park	24c Schererville Indiana	24d Feb10, 2001

FUNERAL HOME	NAME	STREET AND NUMBER OR R F D	CITY OR TOWN	STATE	ZIP
25a. Affiliated Mortuary Service,Ltd.		3552 N. Southport Ave.	Chicago, Il.		60657

FUNERAL DIRECTOR'S SIGNATURE	FUNERAL DIRECTOR'S ILLINOIS LICENSE NUMBER
25b. ▶ *Michaul Bech*	25c. 14401

LOCAL REGISTRAR'S SIGNATURE	DATE FILED BY LOCAL REGISTRAR (MONTH, DAY, YEAR)
26a. ▶ *John L. Wilhelm, M.D.*	26b. FEB 08 2001

VR200 (Rev 5/89)   Illinois Department of Public Health—Division of Vital Records   (BASED ON 1989 U.S. STANDARD CERTIFICATE)

Appendix 7

O F COURSE, MANY PEOPLE do not know the Hyles family. Two sides were represented at the funeral—Aunt Ene's (Earlyne Stephens) side and Dad's side of the family.

Mrs. Earlyne Stephens, my aunt, Dad's sister
　　Athie Denny and Margaret Taylor, my aunt's twin daughters and Dad's nieces
　　Mrs. Stephens' grandchildren and great-grandchildren:
　　　　Vicki Denny Knowles
　　　　Bill Oats
　　　　Sandy Hirtle
　　　　Donny and Cindy Crutcher
　　　　　　Dana Crutcher
　　　　Eddie Paul Oats
　　　　　　Michael Oats
　　　　　　Melissa Oats

Dr. and Mrs. Jack Hyles
　　Tim and Becky Hyles Smith
　　　　Steve and Trina Smith Beebe
　　　　Jon and Teresa Smith Horton
　　　　Trent Smith

The Passing Over of Dr. Jack Hyles

Dave and Brenda Hyles
    Amy Hyles
    Bethany Hyles
Linda Hyles Murphrey
    Melissa Murphrey
    Michael Murphrey
Jack and Cindy Hyles Schaap
    Jaclynn Schaap
    Ken Schaap

Mom with Becky, Linda, Cindy, and me

Appendix 8

Dr. Jack Hyles

A GE 74, WENT TO be with his Lord on Tuesday, February 6, 2001, at the University of Chicago Hospitals. Dr. Hyles had suffered a serious heart attack on January 30, 2001. He was admitted to Methodist Hospital Southlake Campus, Merrillville, Indiana, on Tuesday. He was subsequently airlifted to the University of Chicago Hospital at 1:00 A.M. Friday. Dr. Hyles underwent eight hours of open-heart surgery performed by a team of top surgeons and specialists. In spite of heroic attempts by the medical staff, Dr. Hyles was pronounced dead at 9:43 A.M.

Dr. Hyles was born September 25, 1926, in Italy, Texas, to Willis Athey and Coystal Mattie Hyles. He is survived by his wife of 54 years, Beverly; four children, Becky Smith of Texas, David Hyles of Florida, Linda Murphrey of Texas, and Cindy Schaap of Indiana; 11 grandchildren, Trina Beebe, Teresa Horton, Trent Smith, Jamie Hyles, Julie Hyles, Amy Hyles, Bethany Hyles, Melissa Murphrey, Michael Murphrey, Jaclynn Schaap, and Ken Schaap; 4 great-grandchildren; one sister, Earlyne Stephens of Illinois; and a host of other relatives and friends. He was preceded in death by two sisters, Lorene and

The Passing Over of Dr. Jack Hyles

Hazel, and a namesake grandson, Jack David Hyles.

During World War II, Jack Hyles served as a paratrooper with the 82nd Airborne Division.

Dr. Hyles was a graduate of East Texas Baptist College and attended Southwestern Baptist Seminary. He pastored five churches: Marris Chapel Baptist Church, Bogota, Texas; Grange Hall Baptist Church, Marshall, Texas; Southside Baptist Church, Henderson, Texas; Miller Road Baptist Church, Garland, Texas; and the First Baptist Church of Hammond, Indiana, which he pastored for 41 years, from August 1959 to present. He is the author of 49 books and pamphlets. He founded Hammond Baptist Schools in 1970 and Hyles-Anderson College in 1972.

The viewing for Dr. Hyles will be held in the First Baptist Church auditorium, 523 Sibley Street, Hammond, Indiana, on Friday, February 9, beginning at 10:00 A.M. until 6:30 P.M. At 7:00 P.M. on Friday, there will be a memorial service to be attended by all out-of-town guests and friends, all non-First Baptist Church members, and all Hyles-Anderson College students. The viewing will resume after the memorial service and will continue throughout the night until 9:30 A.M. Saturday, February 10. There will then be a funeral service at 10:00 A.M. for the First Baptist Church membership, including all First Baptist young people who are college students.

There will be a private graveside service conducted for the family only.

Flowers may be sent to First Baptist Church, 523 Sibley Street, Hammond, Indiana, 46320.

Dr. Hyles' ministry has touched and influenced the lives of over a million people nationwide as well as untold millions worldwide.

Appendix 9

HE FOLLOWING PAGES explain the order of service as well as those who helped make the memorial service and funeral service for my dad such a sweet and memorable experience for those who attended.

Memorial Service
Dr. Jack Frasure Hyles
Friday, February 9, 2001
7:00 P.M.
First Baptist Church of Hammond, Indiana

———

Officiating . . . . Dr. Wendell Evans
Congregational Song . . . . "Blessed Assurance"
Prayer . . . . Dr. Russell Anderson
"Find Us Faithful" . . . . Redemption Singers*
Congregational Song . . . . "Jesus Loves Even Me"
Speaker . . . . Mrs. Beverly Hyles
"Majestic Sweetness" . . . . Dr. Bill Burr
Speaker . . . . Dr. Ray Young

The Passing Over of Dr. Jack Hyles

Speaker . . . . Dr. Jeff Owens
"The Unclouded Day" . . . . Dr. Bill Burr
Speaker . . . . Dr. David Hyles
Speaker . . . . Dr. Jack Schaap
Scripture and Prayer . . . . Dr. Roy Moffitt
"Only One Life" . . . . Mrs. Barbara Burke
Speaker . . . . Dr. Wendell Evans
Prayer . . . . Dr. Wendell Evans
Bagpipes
Dismissal . . . . Dr. Eddie Lapina

*Robb Foreman, Kathy Long, Dan and Jessica Mohnkern, Christine Santaguida, Sarah Short, Dave Streeter, Ricky Torres, Scott Tremaine, Deb Wilson, Janette Zelasko

Funeral Service
Dr. Jack Frasure Hyles
Saturday, February 10, 2001
10:00 A.M.
First Baptist Church of Hammond, Indiana

Officiating . . . . Dr. Eddie Lapina
Song Leader . . . . Brother Mario Cuozzo
Congregational Song . . . . "Blessed Assurance"
Prayer . . . . Dr. Eddie Lapina
"Here He Comes" . . . . Precious Name Singers*
Congregational Song . . . . . . "When We All Get to Heaven"

Appendixes

Eulogy . . . . Brother Keith McKinney
Speaker . . . . : . . . . Mrs. Beverly Hyles
"Majestic Sweetness" . . . . Dr. Bill Burr
Speaker . . . . Dr. Wendell Evans
Speaker . . . . Dr. Jack Schaap
"The Unclouded Day" . . . . Dr. Bill Burr
Speaker . . . . Dr. David Hyles
Scripture and Prayer . . . . Dr. Johnny Colsten
"The Sun Will Shine Again" . . . . Mrs. Barbara Burke
Speaker . . . . Dr. Eddie Lapina
Prayer . . . . Dr. Eddie Lapina
Bagpipes
Dismissal . . . . Dr. Eddie Lapina

*April Bicknell, Barbara Burke, Chip Dowdey, Rena Fish, Tim Harrell, Michelle Leonard, Vickie Mooney, Jamon Moore, John Rice, Julie Richter, Greg Turner, and Dan Wolfe

Elaine Colsten, organist and Deb Wilson, pianist

Appendix 10

HE FOLLOWING IS AN excerpt from an article that appeared in the Sunday, April 22, 2001, *Times* about Dr. David Jayakar, the cardiac surgeon, who operated on my dad.

———

In March 2000, Dr. Jayakar brought the high-tech "beating heart" bypass surgery to the University of Chicago Hospitals. The new procedure means the surgeon does not have to stop the patient's heart and keep him alive on a heart-lung machine, which has been a traditional part of bypass surgery since 1967.

It takes a high level of both skill and self-confidence for the surgeon, but the patient recovers faster and doesn't have to worry about complications like brain damage or having a stroke. It's also less expensive. While beating heart isn't offered at hospitals in the region, Jayakar has performed the operation more than 100 time since last year at the University of Chicago Hospitals, where he is an assistant professor of cardiac and thoracic surgery. Dr. Jayakar said, "With a beating heart bypass, you have less chance of stroke, lower morbidity, and much less blood transfusions. This is also less invasive and less costly."

In any coronary bypass operation, the surgeon's job is to get

Appendixes

blood past the blockage inside the heart by attaching an artery on the outside. Dr. Jayakar hasn't shied away from difficult cases either. He has operated on patients who already have had heart surgery, on those with various blood diseases, on stroke patients and those with kidney problems, which complicate cardiac surgery.

Appendix 11

All of the materials mentioned in this book are available.

The cassette tape or cd of Brother Hyles' sermon, "The Bush Still Burns," as preached on Tuesday night, January 23, 2001, in Monterey, Mexico, may be obtained by writing to F.B.M.I., 134 E. Joliet Street, Schererville, Indiana, 46375.

The cassette tape of Brother Hyles' sermon "The Other Shore"; a video and audio tape set of the Memorial and Funeral Services for Dr. Jack Hyles; and music for "The Sun Will Shine Again" as found in the book, *Songs by Dr. Hyles and Daughter, Becky Smith*, may be obtained from Hyles Publications, 523 Sibley Street, Hammond, Indiana, 46320.

Additional copies of this book, *The Other Shore* by Dr. Dave Hyles, may be obtained by writing to David Hyles, Pinellas Park Baptist Temple, 4981 - 78th Ave. N., Pinellas Park, Florida, 33781.

An exciting new cd of 14 songs loved by Brother Hyles entitled "The Other Shore," which also includes a new song written by David Hyles about his dad, as well as special sermon clips, is available by contacting David Hyles, Pinellas Park Baptist Temple, 4981 - 78th Ave. N., Pinellas Park, Florida, 33781.

Appendixes

The Other Shore

CHORUS

    The Other Shore is now in sight,
    And very soon I'll take my flight.
    I'll join my loved ones who've gone on before;
    I'm crossing over to the Other Shore.

VERSE 1

    I lift my eyes and look across that river;
    It seems so close, yet seems so far away.
    With one foot here and one foot over yonder,
    I long to go and yet I long to stay.

VERSE 2

    The loved ones here, I know that they will miss me,
    The thought of parting fills my heart with grief.
    Yet on that Shore there awaits a grand reunion
    That fills my tired heart with sweet relief.

VERSE 3

    My Saviour stands on the golden sands of Glory.
    He waits to greet me home when I get there.
    He'll pull my boat onto that shore of Heaven,
    And welcome me to the Home that He's prepared.

VERSE 4

    When I get there I know I'll look back over
    And see my sweetheart I have left alone.
    But one day soon I know I'll see her coming,
    And I will be the first one to greet her Home.

                                         –David Hyles